P9-BZJ-148

THE POSITIVE MANAGER

Steve Buchholz, PhD, Editor

Wilson Learning Corporation

A Wiley Press Book
John Wiley & Sons, Inc.
New York • Chichester • Brisbane • Toronto • Singapore

Library of Congress Cataloging in Publication Data
Main entry under title:

The Positive Manager.

    Includes index.
    1.   Management by objectives.   I. Wilson Learning
Corporation.
HD30.65.P68   1985   658.4'012   84-21008
ISBN 0-471-82359-7 (pbk.)
ISBN 0-471-01081-2 (clo.)

Printed in the United States of America
    86   10   9   8   7   6   5   4

CONTRIBUTORS

Dan Chabot
Wilson Learning Corporation
Eden Prairie, MN

Thomas K. Connellan
The Management Group
Ann Arbor, Michigan

Brad Lashbrook
RESEARCH FELLOW
Wilson Learning Corporation
Eden Prairie, MN

Velma Lashbrook
Wilson Learning Corporation
Eden Prairie, MN

John Wenburg
Strategic Business Services
Eden Prairie, MN

Larry Wilson
Interactive Technology Group
Wilson Learning Corporation
Santa Fe, New Mexico

CONTENTS

INTRODUCTION

I N OFFICES AND FACTORIES AND STORES ALL OVER the country there's an urgent search going on right now. It's the continuing quest for higher productivity, the key to profits. The search is a tough one, but it could be a lot easier if more managers realized that their best resource is their people. Too many managers overlook that very important fact.

Our friend Tim Stone is one middle manager who was not at all aware of the potential of his people when we spoke to him some time ago. Tim complained to us that his company had "tried everything" to raise productivity, with negligible results. "We've put every job on the computer but the window washer's," he said. "We've crammed the offices so full of word processors and VDTs that the place looks like a spaceship. We've opened our doors to a crew of bright-eyed management consultants, and now we have a whole set of new interoffice forms and a 243-page manual telling us how to use them and explaining all the new systems the management people put in. The company's rebuilt its factory in Weston and launched three new products. For a while after each new move, things look good, but then prices of energy and material shoot up, the competition responds, and we're back where we started from."

We could see that Tim and his company had neglected to tap an important potential growth source—their people. It's here that middle-level managers can really get results, because they are directly involved with the employees. Managing, though, is a great deal more than planning work or telling employees what to do. Effective managers respect their associates and employees and know how to motivate them—by helping them realize that they share the company's mission, by rewarding productive work and eliminating the cause of problems, by helping associates set realistic goals, by providing ongoing feedback on performance and by being there with support when it is needed.

Farther on in this book, you'll find a discussion of *mission*. Wilson Learning Corporation, which originated the material in *The Positive Manager*, defines its own mission this way:

**Helping people and organizations
become as much as they can be.**

Since 1978, companies all over the United States have been using the management workshop developed by Wilson Learning called *Managing Growth Resources*. It has met with an enthusiastic reception. Because our seminar goes so far in accomplishing our mission, we saw a need to make the material more widely available. That was the genesis of *The Positive Manager*. Organized, like the original material, around the concept of the management wheel, it's a way for us to bring you detailed information about each new segment of this diagram:

One way we do this is through the device of our prototypical manager, Tim Stone. While Tim might be less aware of the need for a new approach to management than many of our readers are, the ideas he holds at the beginning of the book provide a good basis for the discussion of positive approaches to managing.

For example, from Tim's initial cynicism about his employees, we can go on to define the mission of *The Positive Manager*.

"Potential growth source," he growled when we mentioned it. "Come around some time and see what kind of growth source they are. But don't come at five P.M. on a Friday—or you'll get killed in the stampede out the door."

"Don't you think you should do something about that?" we asked.

"I would if I could. But I wouldn't know how to start. I'm afraid I couldn't do it without some kind of magic formula."

There's no magic formula. People aren't machines; you can't squirt a few words at them the way you'd oil a coupling and expect them to perform better. You've got to learn what works best. The mission of *The Positive Manager* is to show Tim Stone and all other managers who pick up the book how to become as much as they can be—and how to help their companies and employees be the same.

CHAPTER 1

WHAT'S GOTTEN INTO THEM, ANYWAY? NEW WORKERS AND NEW ATTITUDES

"They've got good jobs and they don't want to do them."
   —The manager of an Ohio packing plant
"There's more to life than work."
   —An Indiana truck driver

W HY DON'T THE PLANT MANAGER AND THE TRUCK driver see things the same way? Why was Tim Stone, our middle manager friend, so irate when one of his laid-off employees turned down reinstatement, saying he was getting more satisfaction out of his new job? And that in spite of the fact that the new job paid $100 a week less and required that he commute thirty miles every day. Tim, of course, thought that Arthur King, the former employee, was crazy.

The answer is an important one for any manager. It's vital for managers to know how attitudes have changed, and why; to know what context they're working in.

In the phrase of Alvin Toffler, author of the best-seller *The Third Wave*, Tim and the Ohio manager are Second Wave people, while Arthur King and the trucker are Third Wavers. Unfortunately, the two don't always see things the same way, and right now it's up to the Second Wavers to harness the energies of their predominantly Third Wave environment.

Toffler divides Western development into three revolutionary eras, or *waves*. The first wave, he says, began to wash over this planet about ten thousand years ago, when primitive people stopped being roving hunters, settled down in permanent homes, and began to farm the land.

About three hundred years ago, the Second Wave swept over the globe in the wake of the Industrial Revolution. Machines took over manufacturing chores; workers began to leave the farms and flock to the cities to do the new kind of work that the machines had created. More and more, the products of their work—and the work itself—began to be standardized. And industries became centralized as factories grew larger.

That Second Wave lasted for more than 250 years. Then, just after World War II, with the development of cybernetics and the entry on the scene of the computer, the Third Wave began to roll in. Compared to the slow, placid movement of the first two, the Third Wave was like the tsunami, the tremendous Pacific tidal wave that is set off by an underwater earthquake. The Third Wave rushed in so fast that many Second Wave managers suddenly found their work places filled with people whose Third Wave attitudes baffled them. A gap in understanding developed between bosses and rank-and-file employees—Second Wavers and Third Wavers—and the gap remains unbridged in many companies today. As a manager, regardless of which wave you represent, it is to your advantage to use the power of the Third Wave. *Ride* it; don't try to turn it back to sea.

Second Wave thinking is notably different from Third Wave attitudes, as we saw in the comments of the manager and the truck driver at the head of this chapter. Each wave brought with it a completely new set of values and ideals. A hunter's daily life is very different from a farmer's. The life of a worker tending a machine is hardly like that of a shepherd tending a flock of sheep. Because the work atmosphere, routine, and demands are so different, the workers' habits and customs and mind-sets are different as well.

Many Second Wavers experienced the Great Depression of the 1930s as children or came along early enough to inherit its worst nightmare—the fear of being out of work. Consequently, many Second Wavers believe that you hang on to a job unless someone offers you a better one, and they expect their workers to feel that same way. But today's workers, more and more predominantly Third Wavers, don't feel that way at all. Their memories are not of the depression of the 1930s but of the rebellion of the 1960s—against authority, against rules, against doing something they don't like just because someone tells them they must.

When the Ohio manager grumbled that his people had "good jobs," he put his finger on a key point. It is in their definition of a "good job" that Second and Third Wavers often differ. To some Second Wavers, a good job is one that gives you a living, with chances for raises if you do your work, and reasonable security. Having experienced at first or second hand the despair of extended unemployment, they are unlikely to fret because their jobs don't provide personal fulfillment or because they get no feeling of having made a contribution to society.

Second Wavers know what their responsibilities are: come to work on time; work conscientiously, keeping at it even though it may be boring or senseless; accept the fact that the people at the very top make the important decisions and then pass them down through a chain of command. That workers should have some say in these decisions is an idea that has come along with the Third Wave. And, because it is a *good* idea, most Second Wave managers have been—and should be—willing to embrace it.

The pattern of decision-making is not the only one that the Third Wavers have challenged. The old get-to-work-on-time rule has also received a pounding from this tsunami. "Why work nine to five?" the new wave people ask. "Why not work part-time or even flex-time? Why not work different hours even on the same shifts? What difference does it make if one person comes in at nine-thirty and another at ten-fifteen?" This idea seemed revolutionary a few years ago. Nowadays it's working well in many large companies.

The organizations that are sparking America's strong return to the world leadership we lost in the fifties and sixties are doing so by using ingenuity and energy rather than depending on taxation or supply-side economics. They know that the real key to improved productivity is employee involvement. An attitude survey of the employees of an American automobile company a few years ago found that the workers felt they were giving less than half of themselves and their energy to the job. Beginning in 1983, organizations within the company have been streamlined, and quality of work has been made the primary goal. As a direct result, most recent surveys have shown an increase of 20 percent in the amount of involvement employees see themselves as giving to their jobs.

But it's the smaller companies, the entrepreneurial organizations, that are leading the way. They've set up smaller work units with more employee participation, and they're the ones largely responsible for the increase in the work force. The *Fortune* 1000 companies actually have fewer employees today than they did ten years ago.

Third Wavers' lives aren't centered on their jobs. They don't think of themselves first as welders or flight attendants or clerks; they think of themselves as people who in sum are a lot more than simply what what they do for a living. Unless their jobs have been made genuinely challenging and meaningful, with fair rewards and the chance to interact with others and to grow psychologically, they're likely to work hardest at outside activities— hobbies, sports, local politics, even their own business sidelines—everything but their jobs.

What does this really mean for managers? It means that employees want responsibility; they need purpose in their jobs. They need to be needed. They can become responsible for themselves, and they must have the opportunity to do so. If management doesn't involve them, they'll leave. There's a whole new value system in the work place, and the quality of the work is what counts.

No one thing caused these changes. A number of influences combined after the Second World War to create the new work atmosphere. The women's movement is one example: more women in the job market, higher family income, less dependence on the man's paycheck. The result was more people in the middle class, expecting more, buying more, and wanting more. When people don't have to be concerned only with keeping a roof over their heads and food on their tables, they not only want and buy more *things*, they start to think about getting more intangible satisfaction out of life—in the job as well as out of it.

There are other reasons as well for the new attitude of younger workers—the baby boom of the fifties, which thirty years later created a huge demand for goods of all kinds, all bought on credit, all helping to push up the inflation rate. A large number of Third Wave middle-class children have higher educations and are unwilling to accept dull, dead-end jobs. They want good pay and satisfaction in return for the work they do.

Then there is the work itself. In the frantic scrabble for higher productivity, all kinds of jobs have been broken down into smaller and smaller parts, so that each worker, in an office or in a factory, has become a specialist in one tiny operation or two out of a possible hundred. It's unlikely that the worker will share the company's pride in a product so far removed from what he or she contributed to it that there doesn't seem to be any connection at all.

There will always be unmotivated people, of course, and workers, young or old, who think the world owes them a living. With the government providing benefits that people never had before—Social Security, Medicare, unemployment compensation—there will always be some who say, "Why should I work?"

That attitude, too, has its roots in the Great Depression, but it has been transformed by the Third Wave point of view. When people with college degrees were selling apples on the street to stay alive, the government *had* to step in. Now it's common for the children and grandchildren of those apple sellers to see financial aid from Uncle Sam as an alternative to holding down a job. But most people won't avoid work if it's rewarding. And very few actually prefer to loaf all the time; most only want an alternative to work because the jobs they have don't answer their needs. Studies have shown that over and over. You can't make people love their jobs—but you *can* make their jobs more lovable.

The psychologist Frederick Herzberg insists that you've got to love your work in order to do it well. "When a worker turns out poor quality work or shoddy craftsmanship," he writes, "he's actually saying, 'I did not love it, so I did not have to be fair with my supervisor or my employer or even the customer.' A human being needs to love his work."

Managers are often alarmed when faced with the challenge of making their employees love their jobs, but their alarm is unnecessary much of the time. The threat of dismissal used to be enough to control the behavior of employees on the job. That threat doesn't work anymore, though, what with big unions, laws that protect jobs, Social Security, unemployment insurance, and a spouse who brings in another paycheck. Managers aren't dealing with poor workers living in fear and trembling because they could lose their jobs. Today's managers must find some other way to influence people, keeping in mind the new attitudes of the Third Wavers.

A survey made by a major American bank came up with some interesting—and instructive—results. Employees were asked, "If you had a million dollars, would you still work?" The majority said yes. Then they were asked, "Would you continue to work at your present job?" The majority said, "No way!" What kind of work would they do? The almost unanimous answer was that they would work to serve their fellow human beings, helping to solve problems and making this a better world to live in.

It's possible to provide at least a good part of that kind of motivation to employees who *don't* have "all the money in the world," who must work for a living. In the new value system, employees can be proud of their organizations and of the products or services they sell. American business organizations do have purpose; the work in them is genuinely meaningful, because the products and services they sell really do serve the people of the country and the world.

"As today's manager, you have to satisfy your workers' needs," I told Tim, "and at the same time you must make good use of their tremendous energy. Learn to persuade. Learn to negotiate. And learn to use the management wheel."

MISSION holds the answer to "Why are we here?"
GOALS answers "Where am I going?"
FEEDBACK is the answer for "How am I doing?"
REWARDS tells the questioner "What's in it for me?"
SUPPORT answers the question "What happens when I need help?"

With the five ideas on the management wheel as the foundation, a manager can turn a faltering department or division—or whole company—into a high-performance organization.

We seem to know, to feel it, when we are in the presence of a high-performance work unit. There is that excitement, the energy, the caring. It is hard to describe, but we feel it; the enthusiasm captures us. Similarly, the marginal-performance work unit is depressing. We see little enjoyment, low energy, somber attitudes. Yet the people in the two work units are not basically different. Researchers have struggled for years to measure that elusive difference. That's what this book is all about.

The people who have done the research, who have contributed mightily are Dr. Steve Buchholz, Dan Chabot, Dr. Tom Connellan, Dr. Brad

Lashbrook, Dr. John Wenburg, Larry Wilson, and all their associates at Wilson Learning. But most of all, the companies that cooperated, provided the test audiences, and supplied the empirical data on which the book is based have made a major contribution.

If you look at any two companies that are alike, except that one shows a significantly higher performance that the other, it's almost a sure bet that the workers in the high-performance company know the answers to the five questions on the management wheel.

In the rest of this book, we'll discuss the answers to those questions in detail, because those are the basics of good management.

Let's get behind the wheel!

Talking It Out

Two longtime managers at the Wright-Jones Corporation, a successful farm machinery manufacturing company in the Midwest, are winding up a discussion of scheduling procedures.

ARTHUR I'm still not convinced that you're right about this flex-time business, Steve. I'll go along with it, of course, because all of the rest of you want to try it, but I just don't like the sound of it.

STEVE Exactly what is it that bothers you so much about flex-time, Art? A great many of our people will benefit from it.

ARTHUR Yes, of course, it'll be just great for them. They'll be able to work whatever crazy hours they want to, but those of us on the management level will go out of our minds trying to figure out whether our people are actually putting in the number of hours they're getting paid for.

STEVE All the studies show that flex-time works very well. When people are happy with their schedules, they don't feel any need to skip out early or come in late. People won't sneak out at four-fifteen to miss the rush-hour traffic if they're working from seven to three or from noon to eight. And they won't come in half an hour late because of traffic jams if they're working from eleven until seven. This new policy will make life easier on everybody — including you, Arthur. You've always been a morning person. From now on, if you want to start working at dawn, you can, and you won't be the only one in the building. Other people get up early, too, so you can all keep one another company.

ARTHUR I suppose you've got a point there, but this business of coddling the employees just goes against the grain with me. These people have good jobs with fair pay and excellent working conditions. It seems to me they should be happy to work for Wright-Jones, but instead, they're asking for more convenient schedules and more decision-making power. When I started on the production line here twenty-five years ago—I was about ten feet down the line from you, if I remember correctly—every one of us was thrilled to have any job at all in a good plant like this. Wright-Jones was a fine place to work back then, and it still is, so why is everybody screaming for more responsibility, more voice in production decisions, more this, more that?

STEVE   Today's workers take good salary and working conditions for granted, Art. They want—and need—something more than we asked for all those years ago. Things have changed since you and I started working here; people are different now. They don't simply want to collect a paycheck every week or two. They want to be part of a worthwhile effort.

ARTHUR   But they already <u>are</u> part of a worthwhile effort, aren't they? Everybody here contributes to the production of the farm machinery that comes out of this place, and each worker is well paid for the effort.

STEVE   But that's not enough anymore, Arthur. When you and I started working, people just wanted to earn a living. In those days you learned that you should get a job and hang on to it until someone offered you a better-paying job with greater security. Our parents learned that lesson during the depression and we picked it up from them. But today's workers don't think that way. They're better educated than we were and more mobile as well. In fact, they're willing and able to move on to just about any part of the country to find the job that will satisfy them and make them feel that they're using their brains and making a contribution to the greater good. If we want to keep these people, we're going to have to recognize their need to use their time and their intellects and their imaginations at peak efficiency.

ARTHUR   I suppose you're right, but I'm finding it hard to adjust to this new world we live in. Like it or not, though, I see more evidence of change every day. In fact, just a few days ago I lost a good man because of this new attitude you talk so much about. One of my best designers left to go to work for less money at a company where he'll be allowed to stay with a design from the drafting table to the wheat fields—all the way with the machine, instead of working on just one step for each different machine. I felt terrible when he told me why he was leaving. You know, Steve, it simply never occurred to me to offer my people that sort of opportunity. Yet when he told me about it, I could see how exciting that kind of work would be. It made me do a lot of long, hard thinking about the way I run my department.

STEVE   Why not talk with the other designers and see how they feel about working that way? When you first moved into designing, that idea wouldn't have occurred to you, because things simply weren't done that way in those days, but it sounds like an idea that would be as good for the company as it would be for the designers. Just think of the degree of commitment we could get from a designer who could work with a combine or a thrasher all the way from concept to utilization. You see, Arthur, these new people do have some wonderful ideas if you just give them a chance to talk them out.

ARTHUR   I'll tell you something else, Steve—mind you, now, I still don't like this flex-time nonsense, but I'm willing to admit that some of the new ideas are pretty good. Something happened recently that opened my eyes up to another mistake I've been making for years. You know, Margaret Anthony has been my secretary ever since I moved into management ten years ago, and she's one of the best in the business. Now, I've always spent the first couple of hours each morning reading all my correspondence and dictating answers for Margaret to type. It was a damn nuisance, but I figured it was just another necessary task I had to perform every day. Well, a few weeks ago I got piled up to the ceiling with much more important work, and I simply lost my patience with the daily correspondence. So I picked up a big stack of letters and handed them to Margaret. "I'm not even going to read these,' I told her. "I hate to burden you with extra work, Margaret, but I want you to answer these letters for me and sign your name over the line 'Secretary to Arthur Trust.' If you find anything you can't handle, put it aside for me to deal with when I have time."

STEVE   If I know Margaret, that stack of letters got answered neatly and politely in half the time it would have taken you to dictate answers for her to type up.

ARTHUR   More like one-quarter of the time, Steve. And that was only the beginning of the time-saving. Do you know what's happening now as a result of those letters she wrote? All those people she corresponded with are now calling and asking to talk to her instead of me, and she handles those calls with all the savvy of a career diplomat, referring people on to me only in matters that are beyond her experience. Do you have any idea how much time that saves me? I hate to think of all the hours I've wasted by assuming I had to do everything myself.

STEVE   And what about Margaret? Did she resent the extra work?

ARTHUR   Of course not. The next day I didn't even have to ask for her help. She answered most of my letters before they reached my desk. In fact, she loves doing it. And I love being out from under that load of correspondence every morning. To tell you the truth, I think that one decision to give Margaret more responsibility has changed my outlook on the way I manage my people—that and the designer who quit on me. Next thing I know I'll be letting you talk me into attending one of those management seminars you're always talking about.

STEVE   Any time you're ready, Art, I'd love to take you along. I think you'd enjoy them. Meanwhile, though, I suggest that you start talking to your designers about extending their involvement with one particular machine instead of working on just a single part of each different item. You might find that you can work out a way to make their jobs more satisfying. And that would make your own job more pleasant, wouldn't it?

ARTHUR   It sure would. But I still have my doubts about this flex-time business.

STEVE   But you'll give it a chance, right?

ARTHUR   Right. I think I'm going to have to give a lot of new ideas a chance from now on.

CHAPTER 2

WHY ARE WE HERE? MANAGING THROUGH THE INFLUENCE OF MISSION

"Why, if a fish came to me and told me he was going on a journey, I should say, 'With what porpoise'?"

"Don't you mean 'purpose'?" said Alice.

"I mean what I say," the Mock Turtle replied in an offended tone.

Lewis Carroll—Alice's Adventures in Wonderland

Every BUSINESS ENTERPRISE HAS A PURPOSE. DOES this statement seem so obvious that it's foolish to make it? A lot of people think so, but that's because they have a mistaken idea of what "purpose" is. To make clear exactly what we are driving at, we will use a different word: "mission."

"Do our customers know that they are our number one priority?" asks an executive of a large department store. "In short, are we living up to our mission?" The chain defines its mission as being in business "to please our customers by having the most wanted merchandise in stock in depth in our stores, by giving them the value they seek in terms of quality merchandise that is both fashion-right and competitively priced." And the chain seeks to carry out this mission—to have every employee carry it out—by giving the customers a total shopping experience that meets their expectations for service, convenience, environmental and ethical standards. Everything they do throughout the organization, they say, should demonstrate, support, and enhance the accomplishment of this mission.

People work for people; they work for leaders, for a cause.

Many top executives are convinced of the importance of mission. Lee Iacocca, perhaps the greatest missionary of all, was able to sell his dream to his vendors, his workers, the unions, the community, even the government. He has a mission, and he explains it very succinctly. You know exactly where he is going and where he wants to go, because he's explained it all to the American public. He sold the consumers, and they bought his dream. America loves heroes, and some of its most effective heroes are the business leaders who have managed to communicate their strong sense of mission to those around them. The people love the Ray Krocs of McDonald's, the Tom Watsons of IBM. These are men who have managed to communicate their strong sense of mission to others.

Mission answers the question, "Why are we here?" for both managers and employees. And the employees, as well as the company and its management, must know and understand that mission. So, first, you—the manager—must understand the company's mission for yourself, and then you must learn how to communicate it successfully to the people whose work you are responsible for. Although the independent attitude of the Third Wavers might make some Second Wave managers uncomfortable, there's another side to the coin. These new workers will be much more enthusiastic about taking on responsibility after you help them see that they play a part in achieving the company's mission.

"What is your company's mission?" we asked our middle manager friend Tim Stone. "Why does your organization exist?"

Tim looked at us pityingly. "That's an easy one," he said. "We exist to make a profit."

But Tim is looking sideways, not straight ahead. We can compare his answer to a waiter's answering the same kind of question—"What is the mission of the work you do?"—by saying, "To get tips."

Naturally the waiter wants to get tips—and Tim's company wants to make a profit. As they say, "We're not in business for our health." But the waiter's *mission* is to provide service that meets the needs of the diners at his tables. If he does that, he will get tips. And if Tim's company fulfills *its* mission, to provide the goods or services that meet the needs of its customers, the company will make a profit. But not unless it does fulfill those needs—or not for long.

Making a profit, getting tips—these are *objectives*. They are what the person or organization on the selling side hopes to gain. *Mission*, on the other hand, expresses what the seller is offering for the buyer's gain.

A company's mission is to provide the goods and/or services that answer the needs of its customers.

The experience of the manager and staff of one of the suburban stores of a retail chain is a perfect example of the importance of mission to any business organization.

A group of young employees, led by the thirty-two-year-old store manager, came to a point where they felt they wanted to improve their performance. They were in competition with similar stores in the chain's operation, and they became more and more aware that they wanted—and needed—to feel that their jobs were more worthwhile, that they were important, not only to the company but to the community as well, and that the work they did made a difference.

It took several meetings and a lot of intense discussion to arrive at a realistic and workable answer to their initial question—Why are we here? The breakthrough to an answer came when they agreed that their purpose should be stated not from their own point of view, but from the customers'.

After that, it was not hard for the employees to define their purpose: They aimed to be the best possible purchasing agent for their area—a fifteen-mile radius around the store that included several Minneapolis suburbs. How to achieve this?

The first thing they did was to study the demographics of the communities they served. As they questioned their customers and got closer to knowing their needs and desires, the employees were able to change their buying strategies. Instead of carrying full lines of merchandise, they became very selective. They stopped carrying both ends of a line and eliminated a lot of items that previously had been stocked as a matter of course.

As changes were made, the store employees became more and more involved with what they were doing. When they found a new style or product, they brought it to their clientele in a spirit of "Hey, look what we found for you!" Communications became two-way. Not just "Come and buy what we have in our store" but "How do you like it? What else do you need? Have you thought about this?" The employee-customer relation became much more personal, with greater satisfaction to both parties.

The results are there for everyone to see. Not only is this store one of the highest performing units in a high-flying organization, but the close relationship among employees is apparent to the most casual onlooker. The staff has become "family." It shows in the way they treat one another, in how they allow, and indeed support, creativity, and in how they deal with mistakes.

All of us have at some time encountered a high-performance culture that is open, positive, and outwardly focused. It's a pleasure to experience this commonly held combination of assumptions and expectations, even at second hand, and it is what we hope the information in this book will help to create in your own organization.

Mission is the most important part of the management wheel, because it is vital to each of the other four elements of the wheel.

It is also a central statement of purpose that must apply to *every job in the organization.*

Now, it's unlikely that many companies are going to gather their top people around a conference table to hear the chief executive officer announce: "All right, ladies and gentlemen, we are here to define our mission." Yet every successful company has a strong sense of what its mission is and just how it translates into the specifics of the organization's product or services.

"Try this," we suggested to Tim Stone. "What do you think the mission of a company that manufactures color television sets would be?"

"Well, judging from what I want in a set of my own. . ."

"That's just exactly the right way to judge," we told him.

"I'd say the important thing is quality. If they build a set of real quality, one that gives good reception and keeps on giving it, with a minimum of breakdowns or problems, then I'd say they were accomplishing their mission."

"Okay. How about an insurance company?"

"They've got to give me service. I don't want to wait forever for a claim to be adjusted, and I don't want to go through a lot of red tape. Service—that's definitely what an insurance company's mission ought to be."

"And a metal refiner?"

"That's a tough one. I don't really know what I'd want from them."

"Look at it this way. What can a supplier like that provide besides quality and service at a reasonable price? Is there something extra that will give them the jump on their competitors, and benefit their customers? How about improvements? New alloys, new applications?"

Tim nodded. "Yes, that's something a customer would want from a supplier like that."

"Alcoa's advertising slogan is 'We can't wait for tomorrow,' and that does indicate what we've just said. Companies often state their mission—whether they know it or not—in their slogan."

Try your hand at this. Translate the following advertising slogans into a statement that tells how, judging from them, these companies are answering the needs of their customers:

McDonald's: "We do it all for you."
Lawnmobile service: "Cutting your work in half."
Swissair: "We take on the world's most demanding business travelers."

It doesn't take a highly paid advertising copywriter, though, to state an organization's mission. Here's the way one managing director expressed the mission of his company:

> If I had to describe it in one word, I'd pick *reliability.* See, customers want to be able to make plans. Now, our products are part of their plans. They have to know what they can expect. Will the machines operate at peak efficiency, for example? Will the supplies arrive when they're promised? And if a machine goes down, how long before it will go up again? So reliability is something our sales, service, and operations people all can identify with.

And that's an important point—that everyone in the organization can identify with the mission. We'll talk about that a little later on.

The operator of a successful theme park defines his company's mission in one word, too—*fun*. That's what they're selling, and everybody connected with the park knows it and works to make it happen.

Can you state your company's mission in one word? A few words? Keep it short, (from the customer's point of view), and make every word count.

We've said that while a company may not have specifically spelled out its mission to itself, management, at least, is usually aware of it. Sometimes, however, customers' needs change and the company doesn't adjust to the change. That's what happened a few years ago in the American automobile industry.

Ever since Mr. Ford brought out his serviceable, affordable Model T, auto manufacturers had known clearly what their mission was: to provide the cars the public wanted at prices the public could afford. And for many years, they did just that, to the glory of their stockholders' bank accounts—and those of management and the workers as well.

But there came a time when people in this country became aware that their cars were costing them more and more to run. (The gasoline lines of 1970s taught them that, if nothing else did!) As gas prices rose, the public wanted automobiles that got better mileage. Disgusted with traffic jams and the hassle of parking, people felt that smaller cars were part of the solution to those troublesome problems as well. They wanted automobiles of a more maneuverable size that would still be large enough to accommodate their families and their gear.

That's what they wanted. What they got, however, was the very large cars that had been popular for so many years.

Abroad, where fuel has always been expensive, car manufacturers were answering the needs of *their* customers. They had been making smaller, lighter vehicles for a long time.

The result? We all know what it was. American auto makers lost out to the foreign companies. American drivers bought Toyotas and Volkswagens and Renaults and Volvos while Buicks and Chevrolets and Oldsmobiles gathered dust in the showrooms.

The industry had lost sight of its mission.

Having the mission clearly in mind helps to prevent the unfortunate and unprofitable situation where the customer, the company, and the employee have different ideas about the company's purpose, and where as a result one or two of them gain at the expense of the other. Here's an example:

A customer comes into a department store with a complaint. She tells the clerk at the Returns desk that the garment she bought fell apart at the seams the first time it was cleaned.

"I'm sorry, madam," the clerk says. "I can't do anything about this. You'll have to return it to the salesclerk from whom you bought it."

But the salesclerk is even less helpful. He doesn't even tell the woman where else to go for help; he just says he can't do anything for her. Determined to pursue the matter, the customer asks for the manager. This person shows up after a rather long time and says, "I'm sorry, madam, but you bought this at your own risk. There's nothing we can do about it."

In that story, the employees and the management gang up on the customer; they win, she loses. But customers who lose don't stay customers very long.

A sales representative for a furniture manufacturer has just made a big sale: several pieces of top-of-the-line living room furniture. In the heady enthusiasm of having done such good business, he grandly decides to throw in some extra pieces at a greatly lowered price—a price that is below cost.

In this case, the employee and the customer won, but the company lost. While some kind of "extra" on the company's part was justified by the size of the sale, the sales rep went too far. Here is one final example:

Ofcal Systems is a computer service company that supplies software and other services for administrative functions like payroll and inventory. One of their customers, Cinderella Novelties, recently had them create special-purpose software for their payroll operation, which is large and complex.

After the system was running, Cinderella called in a management consultant who designed an entirely new payroll procedure. Because the original program is no longer applicable, Cinderella wants Ofcal to adjust it for the new procedures, and feels they should do it at no charge, since the basic software already exists and only certain changes (but extensive ones) are necessary.

The resulting meeting between the vice-presidents of Ofcal, the manager of Ofcal's software division, and the customer is an angry one. The manager is firmly opposed to reprogramming the software without charge, but the vice-president ignores his objections and tells the customer that Ofcal will do it. The vice-president believes that the customer is always right.

This is another two-against-one situation: the vice-president and the customer against the manager. The customer will end up liking the software company—but the Ofcal manager will not. The manager feels the vice-president let him down; his superiors don't support him. The customer and the vice-president win; the manager loses.

Whichever way it goes, it does the company no good. A dissatisfied customer, goods sold below cost, an employee overruled when he had a genuine case to make—all of these are bad for the morale of the company. The only healthy situation is one that benefits all the parties.

With a clear mission statement that everyone understands, conflicts like these are much less likely to come up. Mission is just as important to what goes on *inside* the company as to what goes *out from* the company.

Without an accurate idea of the purpose of the organization, a manager can be sidetracked into bulling toward an *objective* without realizing that the objective is in conflict with the company's main purpose.

"You know," Tim said, "I can give you a good example of that. I'll be the teacher this time, okay?"

"Sure. Give and take—that's the best way to learn."

"Well, not long ago a directive came down from the thirty-second floor—that's where top management's offices are—saying in no uncertain terms that they wanted better cash flow from every department. Truth of the matter was, the company had spent a lot of money trying to break into some overseas markets. Our cash position was really sad.

"When our credit manager got the word from on high, she decided to put all the slow-paying customers on a cash-only basis. So what happens? Our best customer happens to be a slow payer. They've been buying from us for nearly ten years—heavy. They run up very big bills, and they always pay them. It just takes them a while to get around to it, that's all. They buy more from us than just about any other customer; we make a lot of money out of them. Or *made*, I should say.

"Because when all of a sudden they're told they've got to pay cash, or else, they shot back a letter that burned our fingers. I'm surprised it didn't shrivel the paper it was written on. The bottom line, of course, was that they were taking their business down the street; we'd had it."

Tim's lesson was clear. Working toward an *objective*—better cash flow—the credit manager lost her sense of mission—keeping a good customer satisfied—with serious results.

Once thought out, the importance of mission to a company becomes obvious. What is less easy to trace is the importance of mission to a company's employees; yet that is the key to good management, good performance, and good productivity.

Everyone who has something to offer the public—from the painter alone in a studio to General Motors—is one half of a two-sided relationship. The customer is the other half. The mission of the painter, and of General Motors, is to answer the needs of the customer. How they do it is particular to each.

It's true that the connection between the artist's mission and the work that he or she finds fulfilling is a very direct one; it is much harder to see that connection in the case of someone in an accounting office or on an assembly line. Not many people in ordinary jobs are as involved in their work as the painter is in the process of creating art. Few have the advantage of being able to see a direct connection between the work they do and the success of the overall mission. But satisfaction in and with the job—a feeling of well-being—depends very much on believing that what you are doing makes sense to you and others.

Abraham Maslow has said that people work for three main reasons: to fulfill their survival needs, to respond to a leader who inspires them and whom they respect and trust, and to gain self-fulfillment—to help a cause, a purpose. In Minnesota, for example, there is a man who has brought to reality his vision of an arboretum—the northernmost such collection of rare trees and shrubs in the world. He's been able to accomplish this because he has communicated his vision to literally hundreds of people who work as volunteers for him, supplementing his meager budget. He has persuaded these people of the value of his purpose.

It is up to the manager to furnish the assembly-line workers and accounting clerks and everyone else with a clear idea of the company's mission and of the employees' contribution to it, and to convince them of the ultimate satisfaction they can gain from their part in the process.

The next step, then, is to communicate the mission.

You may get some help from the advertising slogan we talked about earlier, if your company has a good one. Ads are directed to the public, but they speak to employees as well; they make clear to them what the company is offering their customers and potential customers. Every Avis employee knows what "We try harder" stands for. *They're* the ones doing the trying.

Use every avenue you've got that is already set up to communicate mission:

- first-day orientation sessions
- training courses for new employees
- sales and service incentive plans

- bulletin boards
- in-house newsletter
- meetings, memos, bulletins

There are lots of ways to "talk" to the people in your department; be alert for them.

You'll drive your message home even more effectively if you do it directly, person to person, as well as pinning up items on the bulletin board and the like.

"Just sit them down and let them have it?" Tim asked.

"Well, yes," we told him. "Take the example we've been talking about —the company whose advertising slogan broadcasts its mission. You could start by asking your people if they feel the ads below state the missions of those companies. If the idea of mission is new to them, it will give you a chance to define it for them. As you go down the list, ask for suggestions about what benefits the customer can expect from each company.

Gerber's: "Babies are our business—our only business."
A computer service: "Information at your fingertips."
AT&T: "The system is the solution."
General Electric: "We bring good things to life."
Alcoa: "We can't wait for tomorrow."
Volvo: "A car you can believe in."

Another way to get across the company's mission is to ask the employees to put on the customer's hat. What would the customer expect from your own company? It's a good way to demonstrate the distinction between *objectives*, like making a profit, and *mission*.

Now you've defined mission and thought up some ideas about communicating it to your employees. In the next chapter, we'll put it to work; we'll tie it to the jobs your people do.

Talking It Out

Barry and Jenny are discussing the direction their company's new advertising campaign should take. They work for Phillips Technical Industries, Inc., which manufactures high-tech information systems of various sorts, including both hardware and software.

JENNY   You're right, Barry. We've grown faster in the past year than any other comparable company on the West Coast. Granted, we've all worked hard, our esprit de corps has enhanced our success enormously, and our products are absolutely top-of-the-line. But there's something else at work in this organization, something that sets us above our competitors, both in our own opinion and in the eyes of our customers. If we can put our finger on that elusive quality, we'll have the theme of our new campaign.

BARRY   We need a key word to start from, and we have dozens to choose from: service, quality, reliability, convenience. We could use any one of those qualities. Trouble is, other companies have jumped on words like that. I'd like to find a theme that's unique to Phillips, one that comes closer to whatever it is that makes us more successful than most of our competitors.

JENNY   Okay, let's stop reaching for abstractions for a moment. Instead, let's look at the individuals who work here and try to see what makes them try so hard and pull together so fiercely.

BARRY   Teamwork, excitement, eagerness.

JENNY   You're getting close, Barry. This is an exciting place to work. The products are exciting; so is the field itself; and so are the people who work here.

BARRY   Yes, but we're not trying to sell our employees to the public, Jenny. We want to project a picture of the company as a whole, certainly, but mainly we have to try to persuade people to buy our products—our computers and telecommunications systems and so forth. Those things are exciting to those of us who help produce them, but I don't think that's why people buy our stuff. Sure, it helps to let people know that we're excited about our products, but that's not the quality that has sent us skyrocketing toward the top so quickly.

JENNY   Let's talk about that, then. Why <u>do</u> people come to us? Just
        because they know we make top-quality high-tech products?

BARRY   The quality of the systems is part of our secret, certainly, but I
        think there's more to it. At any rate, it won't do us any good to
        go around shouting about how good our products are. Everybody
        does that. We'll make that clear, of course, but I don't think
        that's why people have singled us out of the crowd. They know
        our stuff is good, but they don't know or want to know all
        about our bubble-memory chip, which is the main reason why
        our products are so good.

JENNY   Or about our quality-control system, which is another reason. I
        agree with you. Do you know what I suspect, Barry? I have a
        hunch that people turn to Phillips because they perceive us as a
        sort of friendly company that makes complicated systems easy
        to use, not intimidating.

BARRY   Friendliness? Okay, let's talk about that. Our software is
        designed to be user-friendly, and it's selling up a storm. You're
        right about it not being intimidating. Our market research
        people are always telling us that a lot of our stuff virtually
        sells itself to people who claim—or used to claim—that they
        hated computers. We more or less converted them to high
        technology by making available to them software and machines
        that don't scare them half to death.

JENNY   Our documentation is a good example of that. It's not full of
        scare words and jargon; as I said before, it's friendly.

BARRY   And look at our sales force, Jenny. Pete chose them because
        they could talk to people who had never used high-tech
        equipment before. Then he and Dave trained them to get across
        to potential customers the fact that our products are easy to
        use, even for people who tend to be initially wary of
        computerization.

JENNY   Our service people have been trained the same way. They know
        our products right down to the chip itself, but they're able to
        talk to users in their own language and explain to them in plain
        English how to avoid problems.

BARRY   Let's start working out an ad campaign revolving around that
        theme—friendliness. We can get across to the public that we at
        Phillips are real people who speak their language and who can
        make available to them a vast trove of information by means of

equipment and software that are friendly and easy to use.

JENNY   We can go beyond that, Barry. Why not make friendliness a sort of company theme—a mission, if you want to call it that. We could develop our ad slogan around that theme and then use it as a statement of the overall purpose, or goal, of Phillips Technical Industries. You know, "Friendly products from friendly people," or some such. A line like that would let the public know what kind of a company we are and at the same time give our own people a mission to keep in mind.

BARRY   I see what you mean. With some sort of a statement about friendliness to hang on to, everybody here will have something to aim for every minute on the job. A receptionist who greets visitors will want to live up the company theme. So will the sales and service people. You and I will supervise the creation of friendly magazine ads and TV commercials.

JENNY   The people in the labs and on the production line can be made aware of the kind of products they're putting together and the reason they're so popular.

BARRY   Even employees who might otherwise feel somewhat removed from the products should be able to identify with the friendliness theme. The accounting and bookkeeping people, for instance, will understand that they make it possible for this company to continue to produce friendly systems that help thousands of users; without accurate financial accounting, this company would founder—with or without the top-quality products, the friendly software, and the helpful service staff.

JENNY   Barry, I think we've got something good here. Let's go in and present the idea to Pete.

BARRY   Okay. I'm sure he'll like it. We can bounce ideas off him for a few minutes. Then we'll get started on some specific ideas for the advertising campaign.

JENNY   We'll concentrate on real people in the ads, individuals who use our systems. Our ads won't show huge offices full of display terminals. We'll also avoid showing roomfuls of specially trained people doing complicated things that might make the equipment appear to be too sophisticated for new users. Instead, our ads will show kids and old people and teachers and small-office employees using our products with ease and familiarity.

BARRY   I feel really good about this. Come on, Jenny. Let's go tell Pete.

CHAPTER 3

WHAT'S IT GOT TO DO WITH ME? RELATING MISSION TO THE INDIVIDUAL EMPLOYEE

For want of a battle
  A kingdom was lost.
And all for the want
  Of a horseshoe nail!
  —*Old Rhyme*

SOME EMPLOYEES, SOMEWHAT LIKE THE ARTIST WE mentioned in the last chapter, find it very easy to see the connection between their work and the company's mission. Once they know the real reason the company "is there," they understand why *they* are there, as well.

With this in mind, a large chemical manufacturer, after a recent change in the company's emphasis and a redefinition of their mission, has started a three-tiered program. The company has traditionally emphasized technological expertise. When they made the decision to become more marketing oriented, they instituted a three-tiered program to get everyone in the company involved in defining what this means. They hold meetings of top management, middle management and all the employees to discuss getting closer to their customers, and the question underlying all the discussions is "What contribution can each person in the organization make toward becoming marketing oriented?" A salesperson, for example, knows very well that the job is a lot more than simply a matter of getting a confirmed order. The customer had needs before, during, and after the sale was made—needs that the sales rep has the responsibility to serve. There are other kinds of jobs, too, in which the connection is almost as apparent.

"Sales managers are lucky, then," Tim said. "They don't have to figure out some way to show their people how crunching a lot of numbers here can make some teenager happy on the West Coast! But what do I do with that numbers cruncher, or with someone who works in the typing pool?"

We understand why Tim asks that question. There are often very good reasons why an employee finds it hard to see the job making much sense in the company's overall purpose.

What reasons? It could be that the worker

- is too far removed from the end product
- is in a section of the company concerned with administration rather than with direct service to the customer
- performs such a small part of the total process that relating the two is very difficult
- has a job that is considered—by the worker and/or by others—"insignificant."

Take the typist Tim mentioned. This young woman spends six or seven hours a day at a word processor, turning out reports, letters to suppliers, maybe a speech one of the officers is planning to give. It requires quite a leap of the imagination for her to take pride in satisfying a customer three thousand miles away, increasing the company's profits, and helping to fulfill something as grave-sounding as a "mission."

So Tim is going to have to change—*not* lower, but change—his sights. Instead of trying to relate this young employee's work directly to the company's mission, he's first going to have to determine the mission of his own work unit, and beyond that, his own mission as a manager. It should then be relatively easy to show that employee how her work contributes to the success of the department. After that, Tim could describe the department's part in the company's mission.

We don't suggest that you break out in verse at this point, but the old folk rhyme quoted at the head of this chapter will make very clear how important a seemingly minor element can be in the final event:

For want of a nail a shoe was lost;
For want of a shoe a horse was lost;
For want of a horse a rider was lost;
For want of a rider a battle was lost;
For want of a battle a kingdom was lost—
And all for the want of a horseshoe nail!

The typist contributes to the success of the typing pool, which is necessary to the successful functioning of the department, and so on up to the final mission of the company.

By handling the matter this way, Tim is fulfilling one of the highly worthwhile missions of the manager: helping an employee to realize how important she is to the company. That's an excellent mission for any manager who supervises people.

Can you formulate a mission for yourself as a manager? You needn't stop at one; most managers are "multi-missioned." Your mission must relate to the company's, of course, but it will be specific to your own work and department.

"Okay," said Tim. "I see what you're getting at there, and it makes a lot of sense. But what do I do about someone like George, our accountant? He and his staff input the data for the weekly computer report on accounts receivable. George can't see how he makes the slightest bit of difference to the customer or the company. He claims nobody ever reads his figures and that a four-year-old child could do his job. It's not true, of course. He's good, and his job is important. But I don't think George has ever even *seen* the product we make—and he's been with us for eight years!"

George's case is an example of the second reason we mentioned for an employee's finding it hard to tie the job to the company's purpose. Other people can see that George's work is very important—even vital to the company's success. Tim is going to have to convince him that a chain reaches from accurate receivable records to satisfied customers and increased profits for the company. He can explain to George that nothing antagonizes a customer more than to be billed incorrectly—to be dunned for payments that have already been made, or are are not yet due, or are owed by someone else! Then Tim can help George understand that *he's* the one who makes sure that these embarrassing mistakes almost never happen. That should help George see how significant his work is. Once he sees how he contributes to the company's mission, he's likely to feel a good deal less dissatisfied.

Here's an amusing little ploy to determine a person's level of mission. Ask someone what he or she does. If the answer is framed in terms of activity, the sense of mission is missing. But if the person describes the job in terms of an outcome, that person does have a sense of mission.

Later on, we'll show you how other sections of the management wheel can help you—and Tim—bring to your employees a sense of personal mission.

EATON'S WAY

A while back, Tim mentioned an employee, Arthur King, who preferred to stay in a lower-paying, less conveniently located job because he got more satisfaction from it. Arthur's new job was at an interesting plant, where the managers of Eaton are trying to make their blue-collar employees feel more responsible for their own work. Workers on the factory floor are treated like white-collar workers:

- They're on weekly salary instead of hourly wages.
- They participate in the corporate pension plan.
- They get sick pay.
- They are given a high degree of autonomy; for example, they repair their own equipment, and can switch work stations when it is feasible to do so.

If Arthur King is a typical example—and he is—the experiment has paid off. Productivity is up, and absenteeism is 5½ to 9 percent lower than in the company's other plants.

"I'm convinced that my people would use all their abilities on the job if I could show them how they could do so," Tim said. "But I need some kind of structure to get them going."

Tim is right. People who have a normal, healthy outlook want to do the best they can. They don't really want to coast along in a job that demands an I.Q. 75 points lower than their own. We suggested that Tim consider the quality circles program, which many companies have started to use.

QUALITY CIRCLES

Quality circles are groups of workers—usually small groups—who meet on a regular basis. They smoke out problems in production, analyze them, and come up with ways to solve them.

"That's always been the manager's job," Tim objected.

"Sure it has. But in a lot of places now, the managers are sharing that responsibility with their workers. They've discovered that it's a good trade-off. They're getting a lot more than they're giving up. The fact is that much low-level work is monotonous and repetitive. Daily quality circle meetings offer a challenge to workers whose jobs require them to go through the same operation over and over again. And the meetings provide a good break in the day; everyone goes back to the job refreshed.

"There's another bonus in this for the company," we told Tim. "Management has realized, through experience with the quality circles, that they're now getting better advice about how to solve problems, and they're finding better ways to solve them, too. After all, who understands these problems better than the people who actually do the work?"

"That sounds good," Tim said thoughtfully. "You know, I just might give quality circles a try in my own department. It wouldn't be hard to set them up."

Do you have the equivalent of a quality circle in your section of the company? Do you feel it would be helpful to set one—or some—up?

Before Tim puts quality circles into operation, however, he's got to be sure of one thing. We warned him about it. "If you set up quality circles just to get more productivity out of your employees," we told him, "the system is not going to work. The workers will know you're trying to manipulate them, and the whole thing will blow up in your face. You've got to do it because you want to have more satisfied, better-motivated workers in a more positive work atmosphere. Any increase of productivity will be a by-product, that's all."

As Donald Gilbertson of Control Data has said, "We consider it development of our people, training them in how to work together, solve problems together, and develop themselves. As they do this and work on things that are job-related, good things will come of it. . . . People really do give a damn about their work; the only time they don't is when we in management create a situation where they can't satisfy their motivation."

"In other words," said Tim when he heard this, "the workers are still doing what they want to do—working for their own satisfaction. But now they want to do what the company wants them to do as well."

"That's it. Remember, we said that you can't make your people love their jobs, but you *can* make their jobs more lovable. This is one way of doing it. Eaton's way is another. And there are other variations on those same themes: for example, giving the employee a larger share in the planning process and treating the workers like responsible people, which the majority of them are."

"Sounds like a good idea," Tim said.

It is a good idea, and it works. You might want to consider the Eaton experiment and the quality circle method, and formulate a program based on one or both of these ideas that will work for you. If you have more responsible, more satisfied workers, you will get more from them. But remember, if your attitude is "Here's a lollipop; now work harder," you'll get nowhere. In fact, "lollipops"—in the form of increased pay or privileges—are not very effective ways to motivate workers. At Control Data, for instance, there are no lollipops at all—a dramatic demonstration that the workers regard their satisfaction as a sufficient reward for their contribution to the company's mission.

There's one other problem that could hinder your efforts or even effectively cancel them out, but that might be made to work for you instead. That problem is something we call "work place norms"—the culture of the work place. It's the collection of attitudes and customs and strictures that have arisen in that particular place at that particular time. We'll talk about that next.

Talking It Out

The Van Allen Corporation makes and services small appliances. Michael Stettin, a manager at the company, is breaking in a new assistant. Let's listen in on their conversation.

MIKE   Let's go into my office away from all this noise. I want to know what you think of our operation. Have a seat, Rick, and tell me what your main impression is.

RICK   Astonishment, primarily. Those men and women are working their tails off, but they seem to love what they're doing. Even when they're taking a coffee break, they talk shop. I heard two men discussing ways to improve the quality check on the microwave ovens so as to make sure no item gets through with a faulty defrost function.

MIKE   I asked them to see if they could come up with some ideas on that. A number of ovens did get through with defrost settings that malfunctioned. The people who work on the ovens seemed to me the most logical ones to solve the problem, so I set them at it the other day. They'll iron out that kink a lot quicker than you and I could.

RICK   Is that part of the reason they seem to like their jobs so much? Because you give them a chance to flex their intellectual muscles?

MIKE   I think so. It didn't used to be that way around here. When I moved up to this spot, we had a serious morale problem. We had well-paid, carefully trained people who were going through the motions eight hours a day as if they'd left their brains at home. Their bodies were moving, but their spirit was gone.

RICK   And you got this much of a change just by letting them make some decisions about getting the bugs out of the products?

MIKE   We did more than just give them some problem-solving power. You see, this company manufactures and services home appliances, just like dozens of other companies here in the Sun Belt. We wanted a greater market share, but in order to get it we needed something to pull all of the workers together and get them striving for a degree of excellence in product and service that would let us stand head and shoulders above the crowd.

And we did that by showing them that Van Allen stands for excellence.

RICK   That sounds like an advertising slogan.

MIKE   That's just what it is—and it's absolutely true. Excellence is our product, not just ovens and toasters and electric mixers. Everybody in this organization understands that his or her job contributes to the excellence for which this company is known. Our maintenance crews, our data processors, our receptionists— everybody can contribute to the excellence of the company. And in the four years since we made excellence our mission, our market share has increased by twenty-eight percent.

RICK   I see what you mean. A typist might sit at a word processor all day and never see one of the products, but by doing the very finest possible work, that typist can contribute to the excellence of the Van Allen Company. Right?

MIKE   Exactly. Not every employee can design an electrode rotisserie, but every single person on our staff can contribute to the general excellence of our products and service. Our repair people, for example, go out of their way to make themselves available to owners on the telephone as well as in person. Most of the things that go wrong with small appliances can be fixed by the user after talking with one of our people. The repair person simply tells the user to make a small adjustment and thereby saves the user a trip to an appliance repair center. If the appliance needs the attention of an expert, our repair person offers the names, addresses, and telephone numbers of several repairmen in the user's neighborhood. That gains us the support of the user, and it gives our people the assurance that they are directly helping our customers. It also gets us out from under a load of five-minute repair jobs and leaves our highly trained people free to concentrate on overhauls and major repairs.

RICK   Then you concentrate on this mission of yours—excellence—and you don't do a lot of talking about productivity?

MIKE   We never talk about productivity, because we don't have to. Our people are motivated to perform at the top of their ability. As a result, they're extremely productive and the quality of their work is superb. I think that if you have to keep hammering in the importance of productivity, maybe you make people feel they have to keep cranking out more and more items. If you talk about excellence—if you make excellence the mission of the company and the personal mission of everyone who works for the company—then you'll get productivity without ever having to insist on it.

RICK You said this company had a morale problem a few years ago. How did you solve that problem—just by making the mission clear to everyone?

MIKE That was part of our strategy. We also adopted a feedback system; we implemented a call-in procedure whereby users of our products dial a toll-free number provided in their appliance manuals. They tell us what's wrong or right with the product. Many of them make suggestions about how we can improve the next model, and lots of those suggestions are so good that we implement them. The people who take the calls write up a report every week and distribute it to the supervisors, who make the information available to the people in their departments. They discuss the suggestions at length, and the supervisors praise their people for bringing in so many compliments. This system keeps all of us aware that there are thousands of people out there enjoying the products we make, and that those people are as eager as we are to increase the quality of those products.

RICK And that's all a reflection of what you refer to as the company's mission, isn't it? It's one more tactic for helping everybody in this organization see how he or she can contribute to the excellence of the corporation.

MIKE That's right. Getting the mission clear in your own mind is an important first step toward company success. Once you've done that, you can make sure that everybody in the organization understands the mission and the way in which he or she can contribute to it. That accomplished, you'll find that a good many small problems will solve themselves.

CHAPTER 4

EVERYBODY'S DOIN' IT: MANAGING THROUGH THE INFLUENCE OF CULTURE

"But, Mom, all the kids do it."

—*Any teenager you can name*

W E REMARKED TO OUR MIDDLE MANAGER FRIEND, Tim Stone, that teenagers judge one another pretty much according to how well their attitudes and beliefs fit everybody else's. They're careful to do what "everybody" does, wear what "everybody" wears, and even think what "everybody" thinks—"everybody," of course, being the other members of their own small group.

"That's not true only of kids," Tim said. "It's true of just about any group of people. My employees, for instance, think they have to do a job exactly the way all the others do it, even when they know that isn't the best way. Sometimes a guy will hit on a better way of getting something accomplished, and I'll say, 'Great. Let's do it that way from now on.' And you know what he'll answer? 'Why? This is the way everybody else does it, so this must be the way the company wants us to do things.' And *all* of them think like that."

"That idea is what we call a norm—a collective notion that a group holds. Every group of people whose daily life, work, or interests bring them together develops a whole set of these norms, and the pattern they form is called a culture. You'll find all kinds: the adolescent-shopping-mall culture, the weekly bridge culture, the corporation lawyers' culture, the softball diamond culture . . ."

"And the Tim Stone work-place culture," Tim said.

"Of course. The workers in every unit share certain patterns of behavior and attitudes." We explained to Tim that these norms can be productive or counterproductive and may either improve or injure company morale. Either way, these work-place norms influence workers' job satisfaction and determine how well or how poorly they do their jobs.

"It's easy to see why workers conform to these norms," we went on. "As long as people do what the group as a whole believes is right, they will earn the approval of their co-workers. And approval is one reward that everybody wants."

"For sure," Tim said. "You never get too old to want the people around you to accept you as one of them, and you never get rid of the fear of losing their approval."

Tim is right. Very few people would willingly lose the approval and acceptance of their peers, because acceptance gives them so much satisfaction. It reinforces their sense of identity and makes the world around them seem much more stable. And it keeps people from having doubts about whether their efforts make sense to anyone else. When you know you're accepted as a member of the group, you find it easy to say, "Of course, people think that what I'm doing is valuable. I can tell by the way they treat me."

The members of a work group enforce the norms that exist in their culture. If one member of the group violates a work norm in a somewhat unimportant way, the others will probably show their disapproval and perhaps put some pressure on the dissident to change his or her ways. Here's an example. The drivers who work for a package carrier regularly meet for an early evening drink on payday—always in the same bar at the same time every payday. One day, John, a longtime member of the group, announces that he has taken up running and will no longer be joining them at the bar. Because John has violated a norm that the other drivers consider only moderately important, they'll undoubtedly let him off with a chorus of jeers and a good deal of ridicule.

If a worker violates a norm that others regard as crucial, however, the censure is likely to be more severe. Suppose, for instance, that John becomes so besotted with running that he rushes through his deliveries every day in order to start his run earlier. In his haste, he makes errors, drops packages at the wrong places, causes customers to complain excessively, and generally lowers the performance rating of the whole team of drivers. Will he get off with a few jeers this time? Almost certainly not. The other drivers will lean on him as hard as they feel they have to in order to prevent him from violating one of their most sacred norms: Don't do anything that makes the rest of us look bad.

That example shows how norms cause employees to behave in certain accepted ways *with one another*. But the same norms affect the way people work *for you*, the manager. William Lashbrook, in a study he did for Wilson Learning Corporation, maintains that one of the manager's major concerns is the effect of the work culture on productivity. A worker who is satisfied will perform better than one who is not. So the culture of the work place is a reality you can't ignore. You need to get acquainted with it and learn how to deal with it. In fact, this gives you something you can really sink your teeth into—something concrete that you can do to get your employees to contribute to the company's mission.

The culture of the work place can hurt you or help you; it's up to you to see to it that it works the way you want it to. Negative work norms can destroy morale and can lower productivity; positive norms can lead to worker satisfaction and can improve performance.

A look at any one of a number of large companies will clearly show the characteristics of its culture. Intel, with an extremely high growth rate, can trace much of its vitality to the norms of its work-place culture: openness, freedom to hold dissenting views and to disagree with others—including management—and tangible and intangible rewards to those who make decisions and take action. IBM bases its norms directly on the ideas about human worth set out in a book by founder Thomas Watson. The book contains the creed, the precepts that IBM personnel are supposed to behave by: IBMers

THE POSITIVE MANAGER · 47

don't swear; IBM does not pay for alcohol; IBM employees and management do not criticize competitors or, indeed, any fellow human beings. Companies like 3M and Hewlett-Packard demonstrate, in their cultures, the same close correspondence between beliefs and behavior, and all of their people understand this. Although IBM's norms are specifically stated in Watson's book, the norms in most organizations are merely implied. They are no less strong for that reason, and are passed on from one generation of employees to the next.

You are the one who will determine which way things go. Studies have shown that a manager can influence about two-thirds of the perceptions employees have about their work. The other third is beyond the middle manager's control; they stem from conditions set by people at the top of the organization, by outside considerations, such as the economy, and by the employee's personal life.

In other words, you, as a manager, will play an important part in shaping the culture of your work place. You can do this in three steps:

1. **Identify the norms.** Be on the lookout for norms yourself, and make all of your people aware of them, too. Discuss them together. Then make a list of all the norms you and your people have identified.
2. **Evaluate the norms.** Do they work *for* you and the company? Do they contribute to the company's mission? Or do they lower morale and cause performance to slip?
3. **Change the norms,** if necessary. Strengthen the productive norms, and alter or strive to eliminate the negative norms.

IDENTIFYING THE NORMS

Now let's tackle those three steps one at a time. Your first job is to identify the norms that prevail in your work unit. As you do so, keep these things in mind:

- Some norms may be so subtle that people act on them without realizing it and without ever having put them into words.
- Even a small work group may have a large number of norms.
- Norms are dynamic; they change continuously as work conditions and personnel fluctuate.
- Not every worker is affected by norms in the same way.

To get you started on the task of identifying the norms in your own work unit, we'll give you a list of common work-place norms. Go through it carefully to see if any of these norms are in force in your unit:

- Do the job the way you're told, even if that's not the best way.
- It's okay to come in late every morning.
- Doing good work is all right, but it's not all right to be a company person.
- Always eat breakfast on the company's time.
- People with high-level jobs are allowed more privileges than other workers.
- Never work so fast or so hard that you make your fellow workers look bad by contrast.
- Always *look* busy, even if you haven't any work to do.
- What you know is more important than whom you know.
- The department head who turns back unspent budget dollars at the end of the year just isn't very bright.
- Padding your expense account is okay.
- Never show that you're mad, and never give anybody an argument.
- Never do anything without going through channels.
- The boss says that contributing to the United Fund is voluntary, but he really expects you to make a donation.
- Your supervisor says you don't have to go to certain company affairs, but you'd damn well better go anyhow.
- First one to arrive in the morning makes the coffee.
- Channel all good items through your supervisor so he or she can take credit for them, too.
- Make important requests in typewritten memos; don't rely on oral promises.
- Don't ask; just do it. After it's done, it'll be too late for anyone to say no.

If you have more than one work unit under your supervision, you may notice that the culture of one group differs significantly from that of the others. By contrasting the two work cultures, you'll make it easier to identify the norms at work in each.

Take the employees of a city bank—one group working in one branch, the other in a different office. The facilities are similar, as are the neighborhoods and the customers. Yet the two sets of employees have entirely different work norms. In one branch, the workers bring their lunches from home every day; their counterparts wouldn't dream of doing this and regularly go out to a favorite coffee shop. The employees of the first branch come to work in suits or dark dresses, while in the other office people dress informally. The brown-bag employees talk about their jobs at lunch; the others talk about their families, sports, their home computers.

As you can see, being able to observe more than one group of employees makes it quite simple to identify work norms. But suppose you are not yet in a position to do that; you supervise only one group in a single work place. Don't worry; there are other ways to find your people's norms. One good way is to ask your newest employees what they have noticed. Since they have recently come from different work cultures, they'll see the differences immediately. "At my old job, we never ate breakfast at our desks," one might say. Or "When we had a good idea, we got all the credit for it. We never took it to the boss."

At this point, another difficulty may arise. You may have to convince people to suspend some norms that actually prevent them from discussing norms — a kind of Catch-22 that some writers have called "supernorms." Here are some of them:

- Don't volunteer information.
- Don't talk openly to management about your feelings and ideas.
- Don't say anything embarrassing.
- Be polite, even if it keeps you from saying what you think.
- Don't be critical of the way things are done here.
- Don't take a chance of making a fool of yourself in front of the group.

"How would you handle that?" we asked Tim.

"I'd just do my damnedest to convince my people that all rules are suspended during those discussions, that it's to their advantage to say what they think, and that nothing they say will be held against them. I think they know me well enough to trust me."

Once you've managed to dispense with these supernorms, get on with your discussion of the group's ordinary norms. *Do not express approval or disapproval of the norms* your people mention. Be impartial. List every norm that you or they identify.

EVALUATING THE NORMS

When your list is complete, or reasonably so, move on to the second step: evaluating the norms. Think about each norm in terms of its positive or negative effect. Ask yourself some hard questions. Does this norm increase productivity? Does it help us accomplish the company's mission?

Here's a productive norm: "Try to solve your own problems as they arise." That attitude develops workers' independence and makes the job move faster. Now, here is a negative norm: "Do as little work as you can get away with doing." That attitude defeats the company's purpose.

Discuss the norms further with your people. Ask them which ones they consider good or bad. Evaluate all of the norms on your list in this way. Then divide the list into positive norms that you want to strengthen, and negative norms that you want to change or do away with. That done, you're ready to proceed to the third step.

CHANGING THE NORMS

Having identified the norms of your work place and decided whether they work for or against you, you now must do something about them. By now you probably know which norms you want to get rid of, change, or strengthen, and which new ones you plan to put in force. But where do you start? The best way to change or eliminate negative norms is to start with the least controversial. Look carefully at the norms you've listed as unproductive, the negative ones. Which one is the most likely to cause controversy when you change it? Which one will probably stir up the least amount of trouble?

Suppose that your list of negative norms includes these two: (1) wear any old thing you want to wear to work, including jeans; and (2) nobody cares if we get to meetings on time, so don't break your neck trying to be prompt. Which of these two norms is the most controversial? In other words, which one do your people feel more strongly about? Let's say that you think this over and talk to your employees about it. Finally you decide that your people are utterly devoted to their jeans and would be up in arms if you asked them to dress more formally. That norm, then, is too controversial for you to work on right now. How about the other one? Again, after considerable thought and discussion, you arrive at the conclusion that you can, without arousing strong passions, ask your people to get to meetings on time. Start, then, with the less controversial norm, the second one.

You might reorganize your list of negative norms at this point. Put the least controversial ones at the top and work down to the ones your people are most likely to resist losing. Then start changing things from the top down. *Gradually.*

Here's one thing to watch out for: How relevant is the norm to present conditions? It may have made sense at one time, but perhaps it no longer does. An example of this is the norm that it's bad not to look busy all the time. In more restrictive times, this was probably very true; management didn't like to see workers sitting around doing nothing. But now we have learned that when a group has been working at high productivity for long periods, some *guilt-free* down time is really good for the workers' health and morale, and ultimately, for the unit's productivity.

As you eliminate some negative norms, find ways to strengthen those that reinforce the accomplishment of mission. As this process goes on, your people will be more willing to contribute suggestions, because they will see this as a group, not a management, project. Your group discussions of norms will themselves become a norm—an accepted custom of the group. Often it will be necessary only to identify the norm and discuss its effect. The employees themselves will eliminate or strengthen it.

THE POSITIVE WORK CULTURE

Keep in mind, as you proceed through these three steps, that your ultimate purpose is to create a positive work culture, one that provides satisfaction to you and your workers while it contributes to the accomplishment of the company's mission.

What are the benefits of a positive work culture? According to a recent poll, a positive work culture helps you and the company by providing workers with four different kinds of satisfaction:

- With themselves
- With the job
- With their co-workers
- With their managers

"That third type of satisfaction is interesting," we told Tim. "Researchers have found that more people leave their jobs because they're having difficulties with their co-workers than because they seek greener pastures."

"Yeah, but there's one big thing I don't understand," Tim said. "I see how effective work norms create a positive work culture, and I see how that leads to worker satisfaction, which is good for me and for my company. But I don't understand how I'm supposed to know whether or not my workers are satisfied. I can't read their minds, after all, so how *can* I find out?"

"All you have to do is listen, Tim. You can get a fairly accurate idea of your workers' satisfaction with their jobs and their work norms by listening to your people talk about their jobs. And at the same time you can learn a few other things about your employees." Here's how we explained this to Tim.

- The most productive workers are those who are very satisfied with their jobs, and talk about how satisfied they are.

- Surprisingly, workers who are not very satisfied, but talk about their dissatisfaction all the time (gripers) are the next most productive workers.
- People who are highly satisfied but don't talk about it are somewhat less productive.
- The workers with the lowest productivity are those who are both dissatisfied and don't talk about it.

Workers talk about five key questions, and their answers depend on how satisfied they are. Here are the questions:

- Why am I here?
- Where am I going?
- How am I doing?
- What's in it for me?
- Can I get help when I need it?

Do those questions sound familiar? Sure they do, because they're straight from the management wheel: mission, goal, feedback, reward, and support. Take another look at those questions. Try to imagine the answers your employees would give to each of them. And as we move on to our discussion of goals, keep in mind that those goals are anchored firmly to what we've just been talking about: mission.

Talking It Out

Two women who were college roommates some seven or eight years ago have met for lunch. Although they work for different companies on opposite sides of town, they keep in close touch. Let's pick up their conversation as the waitress leaves their table.

ELSA   All right, now, explain yourself, Joan. When you told me on the telephone that you're job-hunting again, I couldn't believe it! You were so excited when you landed your job with the Midcoast Bank. And now you want to leave? I can't believe you, Joan. Your job has everything—prestige, high pay, recognition. What more do you want?

JOAN Excitement, adventure, the thrill of taking a risk and winning.

ELSA   In <u>banking</u>? Are you mad?

JOAN   Not at all. Banking can be terribly exciting. It can be full of cliff-hanging suspense and surprise endings. I just happened to choose the wrong bank, that's all. Midcoast is too conservative for me.

ELSA   Too conservative? Since when have you been a radical?

JOAN   I'm not talking about politics. I'm talking about attitudes, business approaches. Midcoast's bankers won't take financial risks—not even small ones. They insist on playing every game the safest way. Every move they make is designed to advance the client exactly one square forward across the board, with no chance of meeting an obstacle. I want to take a chance on making tremendous leaps forward at great speed, even if it means risking a setback or a block. At Midcoast, nobody takes risks; nobody hits the jackpot; nobody ever gets excited. As a matter of fact, nobody ever wears any color except gray or navy blue.

ELSA   You're wearing yellow.

JOAN   That's my point, I guess. Or part of it, anyway. I simply don't fit in at Midcoast.

ELSA   But you wanted that job so much a few years ago. You went on and on about what a successful bank it is.

JOAN   That hasn't changed; I have. Midcoast is terrific for customers who are satisfied with earning minimum returns on their money at virtually no risk. But that's not the way I want to operate from now on. The more I learn about banking, the more I want to see my clients double and triple their investments—fast. I want to accept huge challenges. Midcoast has been a great training ground, but now I need to find a sort of modern-day merchant-banking organization.

ELSA   You're confusing me. . . . Here's our lunch. Eat something; maybe it'll clear your head.

JOAN   My head is clear, but I can't put my ideas to use at Midcoast. They think I'm a flake, I suppose, but I'm not. I'm just not a Midcoast type. I want to back adventurous clients, people who are willing to take a chance, and I want to work among bankers who say, "Okay, there's a possibility that we could lose a bundle on this investment, but we think there's an even better chance that we'll <u>earn</u> a bigger bundle."

ELSA   You know, I'm beginning to understand you. Now that I think about it, you always did take chances, and you still do. You took a chance on this unknown restaurant, for instance, and the food is great.

JOAN   I found it by accident. Nobody else from Midcoast would be caught dead here. Too unusual. Everybody there is as conservative as the bank itself—in their business attitudes and in their personal lives as well, as far as I can see.

ELSA   That just makes sense, Joan. People who go to work for a company like Midcoast have to fit in with the style of the work place, or they won't stay on. You don't fit, so you want to leave, and I'll bet others like you have left after a short time for the same reason. But the more conservative employees stay, because the bank suits them. In other words, conservatism is the norm in that work place. Everybody there approves of conservatism and takes it for granted. People like you don't fit in, so they eventually leave. Those who choose to remain behind reinforce the conservative norm.

JOAN   It's kind of like Darwin's natural selection, right?

ELSA   Right. Those who can adapt to the environment survive and grow stronger; those who don't are driven out.

JOAN   But I'm not being driven out, you know. I'm choosing to seek a livelier work place.

ELSA   Let's order coffee and continue this. Now that I understand what's bothering you, I guess I agree with your decision to change jobs. Have you done any looking around?

JOAN   I visited a bank yesterday that backs a number of high-tech outfits whose products are so new and exciting that they could change our whole communications system—or they could sink like a stone. That bank hums with tension. Nobody ever sits still.

ELSA   Whereas at Midcoast, nobody ever moves, is that what you're saying?

JOAN   Exactly. All those pleasant gray people sitting quietly at their gray desks, murmuring into their gray telephones. That's not for me.

ELSA   Have you looked at more than one job possibility?

JOAN   Yes. Last week I went to see a sort of merchant banking company that has a number of conservative clients but also backs quite a few unusual entrepreneurs—motion picture producers, racehorse owners, inventors, people like that.

ELSA   Ah, the glint has returned to your eye. What is the work place norm in that bank?

JOAN   Everybody is different—gray suits, yellow dresses, young people, older people, conservatives, flashy types. At that bank, I could be myself and do the kind of work I have in mind.

ELSA   Sounds as if you've found a norm you can live with. I wish you luck.

CHAPTER 5

WHERE AM I GOING? MANAGING THROUGH THE INFLUENCE OF GOALS

"The convict's stroke of the pick is not the same as the prospector's."

—Antoine de St.-Exupery

REMEMBER THE LITTLE DANCE WALTER HUSTON DID in *The Treasure of the Sierra Madre* when he discovered gold? He played a prospector, a man with a goal that meant everything to him, and his joy at reaching it touched everyone in the audience.

The typical cartoon version of a convict, dressed in striped coveralls and cap, swinging a pick over a pile of rocks, shows someone performing basically the same actions as the prospector, but the prisoner has no goal—except to get to the end of the day so he can stop swinging that pick. We'd bet a pot of gold that the prospector will swing his pick a good deal more efficiently—and enthusiastically—than the convict does. The prospector has a goal that he considers worthwhile; the convict swings the pick only because he has no alternative.

More and more companies are setting expressed goals and finding ways to implement them. One leading automobile company, challenged by competition from Japan, determined that only two things were really important for their success: market share and customer satisfaction. (One of these, of course, leads to the other in a beneficial feedback process.) Along with improving the technical quality of their cars, they became much more sensitive to the customers' wants. To learn what these were, and just how the company was satisfying them, they sent out questionnaires every month, starting in 1959, to new owners of their cars and to those customers who had their cars serviced at their dealerships after the warranty had expired. Their goal was to satisfy 90 percent of their customers, and although the exact figures are proprietary, the 90 percent goal is not unrealistic.

Other business leaders pursue a similar policy: two leading makers of data and word processing equipment have "satisfied customers" as their goal as well, and they also keep themselves informed about how well they are reaching their goal by going to their customers at least once a year. One major international air carrier sees load factor as its major goal. All of the employees in that company know that improved load factor is the major goal, and know, as well, what part they play in contributing to the realization of that goal.

All of these companies are managing through the influence of goals.

GOALS SHOULD BE PERSONALLY IMPORTANT TO THE EMPLOYEE

Let's take another look at the management wheel. We've explored the idea of mission—"Why are we here?"—which lies at the hub of the wheel.

Now let's consider the outside section labeled Goals, which asks, "Where are we going?"

It makes sense to set a goal *before* you start on any kind of project. (Always keep in mind that the question is "Where am I going?" Don't let it turn into "Where is all this leading me, anyhow?")

"My experience with goals," Tim Stone said, "is secondhand. Top management sets them and then hands them down to me—and believe me, I don't think much of top management's goals."

"Why?" we asked him. "What's wrong with management's goals?"

"Plenty."

We badgered Tim until he listed six weaknesses in the goals set by top management.

"First," he said, *"the goals are too general.* They put me in mind of the story about the catcher who goes out to the mound when the bases are loaded. The tying run is on third, and the other team's .385 hitter is up. So the catcher says to the pitcher, 'Strike him out!' Management does the same thing. It says, 'Sell more toasters' or 'Make fewer delivery errors,' when it *should* say, 'Sell seven more toasters in May than you sold in April,' or 'Double-check every shipment before it leaves the warehouse.'

"And second, the goals are *not realistic.* Sometimes it seems to me that those guys up there haven't the faintest idea whether we can turn out five units in an hour or five hundred! They should do their homework, find out how much we now produce, and *then* set a goal slightly higher than current production.

"Third, management's goals are *not negotiable.* They're set up in such a way that we can't adapt them to the individual person or situation. We want to be able to say, 'We'll sell *eight* more toasters in May, but we can't double-check the orders unless you let us hire another guy. Deal?'

"Fourth, some goals *conflict with others* that are just as important. If we aim for one, we're going to make it impossible to reach the other. For instance, management says we have to cut our customer-entertainment expenses by twenty percent, but *at the same time* it says we have to bring in fifteen percent more customers in the next two years. Now, how can we get new customers if we don't spring for a dinner now and then?

"Fifth, the goals are *not flexible* enough. Sometimes they're the same for everybody when they shouldn't be, and sometimes they're different for different people when they ought to be the same for everybody.

"And goodness knows, management's goals are seldom clear. A manager says to a subordinate, 'Boost morale in your unit,' for instance. What does *that* mean? Smile a lot? Tell jokes? Let your people take longer breaks?"

"Those are all justified complaints," we told Tim. "And they're the same complaints a lot of other middle managers have. We're going to establish criteria for clear, realistic goals; the goals management sets for you and those you set for your people. But before we get to that, here's one rule you should remember: Like the mission a goal must be *personally* important to the individual employee.

"The job doesn't come first with the employee," we told Tim. "Personal interests come ahead of work. Take that prospector we were talking about. What makes his goal such a powerful force for him?"

"The things he'll buy with his money when he strikes it rich?"

"Well, yes, that's part of it. But the main reason he works so hard is that his goal is a *personal* one; he's working for something that's very important *to him*. At the opposite end of the spectrum we have the man in the striped prison suit, working toward something he couldn't care less about. The rocks he's breaking may be important to the commissioner of roads and highways, but they mean absolutely nothing to the guy swinging the pick.

"The first thing a manager has to do is find out what the personal goals of the employees are. Then he or she can tie those personal aims into the company's goals."

"You mean, so that what's good for the company is good for the workers?"

"That, and vice versa, which we're learning the importance of all the time: *What's good for the workers is good for the company.*"

We asked Tim if he remembered the lower-level jobs he'd had years ago and how he felt about them. After all, none of us started our working lives as managers. We all had lower-level jobs at one time. In fact, a good many of us started out by delivering papers after school in junior high!

He laughed. "When I was in college, I went around trying to get organizations to hold their banquets in the hotel I was working for."

"Did you have a goal then? What was it?"

"I guess my goal was to sell more and more banquet dates."

"For the good of the hotel?" we asked him.

He laughed again. "I don't think I gave a damn about the hotel. I just wanted to see if I could keep on improving my score so I'd get a raise.

"You've got to understand," Tim went on, "back then, nobody asked you whether you liked what you were doing, or what your goals were. Your personal goals were to earn a decent living; that's what you wanted out of your job."

"Not true anymore, is it?"

"Definitely not."

WHAT DO YOUR PEOPLE WANT OUT OF LIFE?

We talked about the Second Wavers and the Third Wavers in an earlier chapter. It might be helpful to bring them up again in connection with this matter of goals. What Tim said about making a decent living—that was certainly true of the Second Wavers. When the Third Wave came rolling in, we heard fewer people saying, "Be glad to earn a living," and more saying, "I want a luxurious home, a fine car, and a college education for my kids." The Third Wavers also wanted the time and money to enjoy leisure activities.

As a result of the arrival of the Third Wave, there's now a different feeling in the work place. "I want to live a full life," today's worker says. "My job is only one part of my life. I expect my employers to give me work that is rewarding and challenging, because I want to feel that I'm doing something worthwhile."

This new attitude forces you, the manager, to learn what your people's personal goals are.

Tim seemed dumbfounded. "How am I going to find out what my people's personal goals are? I can't pry into their secrets. Do you expect me to walk up to my employees and say, 'Tell me what you want out of life'?"

"Bingo," we said.

Ask, by all means. Some managers, granted, will feel uncomfortable talking to their employees about goals. And many employees find it hard to put their goals into words. They couch their ideas in fuzzy, vague words that have little real meaning to anyone—including the person who's talking. "I want to do something worthwhile," someone will say. "I want to serve society."

One way to learn what your people really want out of life is to go beyond the across-the-desk interview. Get to know your employees as people, instead of merely as employees. If possible, join them occasionally for some activity outside the work place—a softball game, perhaps, or some lunchtime window-shopping. Work doesn't set the limits of their world any more than it does your own.

You might want to start by telling your people what *your own* values and goals are. Try it after an evening of bowling, over a beer or a soda; bring it up naturally, if possible, in the discussion over coffee after a movie you've all seen together. Chances are, you'll find that others will follow your lead, talking about their own ambitions and goals.

Getting to know the people you supervise as *people* instead of just *employees* will establish a solid basis for building trust between you and them.

Tim nodded when I told him that. "I know what happens when my people *don't* trust me. They just say what they think I want to hear, and that doesn't do me any good at all. I don't want someone to say, 'My goal is to do everything I can to help the company make money.' Who needs that?"

It's only natural for people to put their personal needs and desires first. Some psychologists tell us that we all share at least three strong personal goals:

- We want to be accepted by those around us.
- We want to be loved.
- We want to feel valuable.

One bonus of opening yourself up to a real give-and-take with your people is the satisfaction you'll have in recognizing that the information you're getting is genuine and worthwhile in improving your own performance as a manager. Once you have the necessary information, you're prepared to set up effective goals for your work unit. As you work out what those goals should be, ask *all* of the following questions about *each* goal:

Is it realistic? If your unit now produces 100 leather pocketbooks each week, are you being unrealistic if you ask your people to increase their production to 200 a week by the end of the month? (Definitely—*very* unrealistic!) Could your people put out 105 pocketbooks a week? (Easily.) Well, now, if they could do it easily, the goal of 105 is unrealistically low, isn't it? Maybe you haven't been challenging your workers. Perhaps you've let them grow lax and bored. Try setting a goal of 115 pocketbooks a week by the end of this month. If they reach that goal, *praise* them and leave them there for a while. Then raise the goal by another 10 and see what happens. Realistic goals, remember, are absolutely key. If the goal is too high, your people will become frustrated and resentful; if it's too low, they'll drift into dissatisfied apathy.

There's a game that has become a classic example of setting realistic goals. It was developed by David McCullough, whose work in achievement motivation is seminal. It's a simple ring-toss game, the object of which is to get two out of four ringers on a peg. You decide how far from the peg you will stand to make a throw, keeping in mind that the closer you stand, the fewer points you get for making the required ringers. You soon learn which distance/point-value is your realistic optimum: neither so far away that it's very unlikely you'll be able to ring the peg (in which case you are likely to give up soon in frustration) nor so close that there is no challenge and very little reward (here again, you'll probably give up trying; it's too easy, too unrewarding, and too uninteresting).

Is it understandable and specific? People have to know what you expect of them. Don't say, "We want better sales." That doesn't provide anybody with a clear goal. Instead, try, "We want 10 percent more sales." That is a clear goal, and it is more likely to motivate people, because it tells them exactly what they're aiming for.

Can you measure your people's progress toward the goal? You should be able to state the goal in concrete ways—in terms of quantity time, cost, and so forth: "Get fifteen more orders by the end of April," for example, or "Save ten percent on inventory in the next month." Only in this way can your workers see whether they are progressing toward the goal or falling behind.

Is your goal related to specific actions that the employee can perform? State your goal in terms of what you want the employee to do, not in terms of the result to be achieved. Telling an airlines worker to "increase your customer satisfaction" isn't specific enough to be meaningful to the worker. Instead, say this: "Tell all of your customers that they can change in Dallas or in Atlanta, whichever they prefer, and then explain the advantages and disadvantages of each switching point." This will give the clerk a specific action to perform.

Have you set a time limit? Your statement of goal should specify not only *what* has to be done but also *when* it must be finished. For instance, your goal might be "to produce 120 electric pencil sharpeners a day *by the end of October.*"

Is your goal written down? Written goals work better than unwritten goals. When people see something typed (*not* scrawled in pencil), they regard it as "real" and "serious." How many times have you yourself said this: "I *know* it's true; it's right here in black and white"?

Is each goal compatible with, not contradictory to, the others? If you want to avoid conflicts between your people and between various departments, you must make certain that one person's goal does not create more work for another worker.

Is the goal acceptable to all of the parties concerned? You won't get good results by imposing goals from above. This means that you may have to spend some time negotiating with your employees and persuading them to help you arrive at goals acceptable both to you and to them.

Are you prepared to keep the goal up to date? Be sure to let the employees know that you are. That way, they won't be afraid of getting stuck in a situation where the goal is no longer realistic.

Does the goal have built-in feedback? There's got to be a way to check on the work as it progresses, so that people working toward the goal can know that they are getting there. We'll discuss feedback in detail in a later chapter.

What will the employees receive when they attain the goal? The type of reward will depend on the job, the goal, the company, and the employees. It could be anything from a pat on the back to a raise or a trip to Europe. Or it could be simply the satisfaction of accomplishment. But, whatever it is, make sure that the employees benefit somehow by reaching the goal.

"Tim," we asked, after going through all this, "do you see the advantage to you of having clear and specific goals for your work unit?"

"Sure," Tim said. "Goals give people a 'destination.' They motivate the workers and show them which direction to take. I can see where they'd act as a kind of milestone, showing me—and the worker—just how well the worker is getting along in the job. Goals should make it easier for me to evaluate individual performance."

"Well, it's a good thing you see all those advantages, Tim, because as a manager, you'll have to be willing to sacrifice something in return for them."

"Come on, now," he protested. "I'm already sacrificing my Saturday afternoons and Tuesday evenings, working out effective goals for my people!"

"That's not the kind of sacrifice we're talking about. You'll also have to sacrifice some of your responsibility, Tim. You see, when you set really effective goals, you give your people a clear understanding of the direction their work is supposed to take. With all that know-how they'll soon be able to take on more and more responsibility. Managers then have to be willing to share some of the decision-making with their employees.

"Remember Arthur King? He came to enjoy his job and do better work when he was given a chance to maintain his own tools, make decisions about getting rid of bottlenecks, and carry more responsibility for other aspects of the job."

"I can see some managers having trouble with that," Tim said. "They're going to feel a little insecure about giving up some of their decision-making power."

"That's right. With more democracy in your workplace, you're going to have to let others make more judgements."

"It's something of a sacrifice, sure," Tim said. "But that's okay. I know if I were in my employees' place, I'd be pleased to be able to make decisions on my own, and I'd work better that way. When we get to that point, though, I'll expect better performance all around."

"I'm sure you'll get it. A lot of companies have tried this kind of goal-setting."

THE RUSHTON EXPERIMENT

We told Tim about one outstanding example: Rushton Mining Company. That company set up an experiment in just one section of the mine, using miners who volunteered to take part. The crew foreman was given a single goal: to be responsible for overall safety in the mine. Each miner was given special safety training, too. Safety was the only thing the foreman was responsible for; he did not supervise any other aspect of the man's work. The miner's new goal was to figure out the best way to do the work, to rotate jobs, and to handle their own grievances. Their reward for reaching this goal was a share in any gains in productivity.

Here's what one worker said after participating in the Rushton experiment for nearly a year:

> We began to feel somebody up there trusting us, and in a week or two we were bustin' our hump in a way I've never seen guys work underground before. When a machine busts down nowadays, most of the time we don't bother to call a maintenance man. We just fix it ourselves, because we feel it's just as much ours as our own car at home....
>
> The foreman, he don't talk like a boss no more, but like a guy down there to protect us—and down there we need all the protection we can get....Before, when the whistle blew, we couldn't wait to get the hell off company property and forget our work. These days sometimes you'll find us up in the shower room half an hour after work, arguing about the problems on the face down below, and what we're gonna do about them tomorrow.

Upper-level managers like it too. Why wouldn't they? In the first year, absenteeism was nearly 75 percent lower in the experimental area than in the rest of the mine; there were half as many accidents and nearly 75 percent fewer safety violations. Supply and maintenance costs were down by 35 percent. The company president says that productivity has increased significantly.

Lower-level managers also like the arrangement, even though their responsibilities have been drastically reduced to safety alone. Like anyone who has ever spent time working on a coal face in the bowels of the earth, with the ever-present possibility of cave-ins and contaminated air, they appreciate how enormously important their single responsibility is.

Rushton's managers did what every manager is supposed to do; they took a hard look at what each worker was doing and then reassigned responsibilities so as to get the greatest possible improvement in performance out of everybody involved. They started by realizing that the mine foreman's most important goal was to ensure the safety of his men. The actual work of extracting the coal became the goal—and, of course, the responsibility—of the miners themselves. By establishing clear, realistic goals—and thereby shifting the workers' responsibilities—Rushton's managers made everyone's job more challenging and rewarding.

Rushton, you see, identified the aspect of each job that was most productive and then encouraged each worker to concentrate on that one task.

THE 20–80 RULE

The Italian economist Vilfredo Pareto, observing that 20 percent of the population of his country held 80 percent of the wealth, decided to investigate a variety of other situations. He came to the interesting conclusion that the 20–80 rule, with certain minor variations in the figures, applied to a large number of other situations as well. As a sales manager, for example, you would very likely find that

- 20 percent of your activities produce 80 percent of your accomplishments
- 20 percent of the sales representatives make 80 percent of the sales
- 20 percent of your product line accounts for 80 percent of your sales
- 20 percent of the customers account for 80 percent of the purchases

Apply the 20–80 rule to situations with which you are familiar and see how often it applies.

The challenge to managers is to find and influence the 20 percent of what their people do that produces 80 percent of the benefits to the company. Remember that managers too often notice and emphasize results but overlook the actions that produce them.

It isn't always easy to pick out the effective actions. Sometimes one small thing will make the difference between high and low performance. Recently, for example, we heard about two insurance salesmen who worked for the same company. Both of them seemed, at first glance, to be equally good sales reps. Both had poise; both were attractive and persuasive; both were persistent without being irritating. Yet one sold 30 percent more policies than the other. Why? To find out, their sales manager supervised them very carefully. He discovered only one real difference in their methods. The less effective salesman wasn't finding out immediately whether or not people could afford the company's policies. As a result, he wasted time on poor sales prospects. He was working very hard—possibly harder than his rival—but he was working at the wrong thing. He was in an "activity trap."

"Here's your homework," we told Tim. "Write the name of your top performer at the top of a sheet of paper and list everything that employee does while on the job. Then take a hard look at that list. Pick out the 20 percent of that employee's actions that you think lead to 80 percent of the results he or she achieves."

The next time we saw Tim, he handed his list to us. "You know what I found?" he said. "The results are easy to list, but it's harder to figure out which action is responsible for them."

Has that been your experience, too? It usually is. As a manager, you naturally focus on the bottom line—results—but it's important for you to begin looking for the actions behind the results. Try the "homework" we gave Tim, and see which actions produce the most results for you.

"Good. You did your homework, and so you've earned a reward," we told Tim.

He laughed. "A gold star on my forehead?"

"Something better. We're going to give you a set of guidelines that will help you set goals for your employees."

"That *is* better than a gold star. If I have a specific plan, it'll be easier for me to get this thing going. Any blueprint or guideline or plan that you can give me to hang on to will help a lot."

"This is really helpful. It's a system called ROI. We'll explain it in the next chapter."

Talking It Out

Goals, as we have seen, must be clearly stated and realistic. They must also be drawn up in such a way as not to create conflicts. Eric and Jeff work in different departments of the same large plastics manufacturing company, and they ride home on the same train. Jeff is happy with his job, but Eric has a number of complaints. His dissatisfaction arises mainly from the fact that his manager never learned the importance of setting goals that do not conflict with one another. This conversation occurs on a commuter train after a day of work.

JEFF   You're upset about something this afternoon, Eric. I can tell by your scowl. What happened? Or should I say what did Leo Hadley do wrong today?

ERIC   Leo always does the same thing wrong, Jeff. You know that. He's a nice guy, but a terrible manager. Wait'll you hear what he did this time. Two months ago—I think I told you this—he asked me to get some long-term contracts on the resins we use. That sounded sensible to me, because we all knew the price of resin was going to shoot up. So when Leo asked me to get shipments from several suppliers, I thought he was making sense, for once. I got right on it and loaded us up with resin at reasonable prices. In fact, I got a couple of the best bargains you ever heard of.

JEFF   Sure. I remember when you mentioned those deals. Seems to me Leo should have been real pleased about them.

ERIC   Wrong. It turned out that Leo, without my knowing it, told Mark Weiss to do exactly the same thing. Of course, he didn't bother to tell Mark that I was also out there acquiring resin by the carload. So what happened was that Mark and I loaded this company up with more resins than we'll need for years and years. Think of all the money we tied up in that stuff—all because Leo never bothered to tell us we were both working toward the same goal. And of course Leo is grumbling at both of us for spreading the company's money around so lavishly, but the whole thing is really his own fault. Leo wasted Mark's time, my time, and the company's money, just because he's too disorganized to get his goals straightened out and keep each of his people informed about what everybody else is up to.

JEFF   He keeps doing things like that. Instead of setting a single goal for both you and Mark so that you could work together, he created a conflict. You and Mark aren't the only ones who are fed up with Leo, you know. I keep hearing horror stories about him from all sorts of people.

ERIC   You hear about him way off in R and D? Don't tell me Leo's reputation has spread that far?

JEFF   It sure has. I was talking to Susan Jacoby the other day in the cafeteria. Did you hear what Leo did to her?

ERIC   No, but I saw her storm out of his office about three days ago. What happened?

JEFF   Seems Leo called her on the carpet some time ago for not bringing in enough orders from our regular customers. He said she'd been concentrating too hard on getting new accounts, and she should ease up on that sort of thing and give her attention to the slow and steady older clients. So that's exactly what she did. She lined up all kinds of sales with the older outfits, sold off carloads of every kind of plastic the company produces.

ERIC   Sounds good so far. I don't see how Leo could complain about that.

JEFF   He did, though. After three weeks or so he called Susan into his office and raised hell because she hadn't brought in enough new customers. He said she'd been spending too much of her time with the same old outfits.

ERIC   No wonder she looked furious when I saw her coming out of his office. He chewed her out for doing exactly what he'd told her to do. Did she remind him that she was following his orders by selling to the older customers?

JEFF   Sure, but Leo said, "I didn't mean <u>forever</u>. I just meant for you to concentrate on the older customers for a few days, a week at the most. You should have known that!" Can you imagine? He expects her to read his mind, maybe? I think he's going to lose her. She's good at her job, and I suspect she'll start looking around for another spot if Leo keeps up his nonsense. He should have sat down with Susan so that the two of them could decide together on how many sales dollars she was to aim for from each group of customers.

ERIC   He pushes us all to the limits of our patience with his contradictory orders and his inability to keep us in touch with one another.

JEFF   He's not the only bad manager around here, though. Did you hear what happened to Nancy O'Brien?

ERIC   The woman who does the newsletter?

JEFF   <u>Did</u> the newsletter. She quit a couple of days ago.

ERIC   How come? Everybody in the company was talking about how much better the newsletter has been since she took it over. It had more real news, it looked better, and it reached several thousand readers because of her circulation campaign.

JEFF   That circulation increase, it turns out, was the problem. Her manager, it seems, told her six months ago to make a big effort to reach another ten thousand or so readers, so Nancy hustled up a whole new mailing list, improved the newsletter, and sent it out to almost forty thousand people—an increase of nearly eleven thousand in the past six months.

ERIC   In other words, she did exactly what her boss told her to do, right?

JEFF   Right. But her boss turned around and promoted another employee over Nancy's head. He was mad because Nancy went over her budget on the newsletter. He pointed out that the extra eleven thousand newsletters cost too much to mail and that the budget wouldn't cover that kind of expense.

ERIC   In other words, her manager is doing the same sort of thing that Leo's been doing. He told her to increase circulation, but when she did exactly that, he penalized her for it by promoting someone else over her head.

JEFF   Mmm. That sort of thing apparently goes on all the time in that department. Nancy said she was tired of trying to reason with her manager and weary of his conflicting demands. She landed a job in a public relations agency where she won't have to put up with that kind of thing.

ERIC   And how about you, Jeff? You never complain about your manager. How come?

JEFF   He doesn't give me any reason to. He keeps in such close touch with all of his people that he knows immediately when one of us is unhappy about something. Then he sits down with us and helps us isolate the problem. Once we've done that, we solve it together.

ERIC   For example?

JEFF   Okay, for example, we have this resident genius named Herb Chernyk who will probably revolutionize the plastics industry all by himself. But Herb is one of these silent types who likes to work alone and <u>hates</u> to train new engineers, which as you know is a responsibility that we all assume on a rotating schedule. Now, I love to train people; I like that better than almost anything. So our manager picked up on that difference between Herb and me right away, without either of us even being aware of it. He called us both in and asked us if we could work out an equitable switch of responsibilities that would allow me to assume Herb's training sessions while Herb took some of the paperwork off my desk.

ERIC   And that's what you did? Herb does the paperwork and you train the new people?

JEFF   Exactly. And it's been working out perfectly. Herb likes to punch data into the computer; I like to feed information into human beings. We're both happy, just as the manager knew we would be.

ERIC   Your manager, then, took the time to study you and Herb, figure out what you did and didn't like to do, and then found a way to make you both more satisfied with your job—by rearranging your goals to suit you better. How lucky can you get?

JEFF   We know we're lucky, especially when we hear stories about Leo Hadley and the other managers. In research and development we just don't have those kinds of problems. Our manager sees to it that his goals, the company's goals, and each employee's goals are compatible with one another and crystal clear to everyone. That way we avoid the kinds of conflicts that occur in other departments.

CHAPTER 6

VIVE LE ROI! A SYSTEM OF GOAL-SETTING

"Provide me with a rack upon which to hang my actions."
—*Anonymous sixteenth-century drama*

THE SYSTEM OF GOAL-SETTING CALLED "ROI" HAS three components:

- Responsibilities
- Objectives
- Indicators

ROI is a spin-off of a procedure called MBO—Management By Objectives—one of the earliest and best-known goal-setting systems. In essence, it consists of two basic steps:

1. You and your employees agree on objectives.
2. You manage the resources of the organization in such a way as to achieve those objectives.

MBO was simple, and when it was used at the management level, it worked pretty well.

"It didn't work so well in my unit," Tim Stone said. "I tried it a few years ago with my people, and the results were zilch."

"That's what a lot of people discovered when they tried it at a nonmanagement level," we told him. "Managers are different from lower-level employees in that they feel sufficiently rewarded simply by achieving an objective they've helped to set. Nonmanagement employees are less likely to think that way; they want tangible, concrete rewards. Managers are close enough to the company's mission to see that the work they do really does contribute to the success of the company, but this isn't true of people who work on the lower levels. Nobody is likely to congratulate the night janitor in a bank for his contribution to the bank's successful year, even though his work really did contribute to that success.

"ROI, on the other hand," we told Tim, "is a system that all of your employees can relate to. Unlike MBO, it can be tailored to the work they themselves do and to the results they produce. They'll keep on evaluating themselves and setting goals, so that they will always have a yardstick against which to judge their performance as they work toward the goal that they themselves have set."

ROI helps you *define the responsibilities* of a job, *set objectives* for each responsibility, and *establish indicators* to measure your progress toward these objectives. Together, you and the employee can easily see whether that person is doing everything he or she must do to get the results you have both agreed are desirable. You and the worker will of course have divided the job into several steps; the ROI system will help you find out whether any of those steps are not being performed—or are being performed unsatisfactorily. Using ROI, you will learn automatically and immediately when it is necessary to have a talk with the employee about ways to do the job better. Without the ROI system you would not even know that counseling was needed, let alone what kind of help to give the employee.

RESPONSIBILITIES

The first step in setting up a ROI system is to draw up a roster of responsibilities for each key area. As an example, here is a list of the responsibilities that a manager in an insurance company might draw up for the agents under his or her supervision:

1. *Marketing:* Locating and qualifying people whom the agent might interest in the products and services the company offers.
2. *Sales:* Working with a prospect to analyze and solve any life insurance or related financial problems that prospect faces.
3. *Service:* Doing all the follow-up tasks after delivering a policy, thus keeping the relationship with the client active and the financial plan up to date.
4. *Management:* Performing all the necessary administrative chores —setting goals, planning, monitoring progress.
5. *Growth:* Working to enhance the agent's own personal and professional growth.

Your mission—your answer to the question "Why are we here?"—is quite likely to become clear to you when you learn what the key areas of your job are. Until you know this, you run the risk of getting into the sticky situation described in an earlier chapter, where the employee, the customer, and the company all interpret the mission differently.

Tim Stone very efficiently avoided such a conflict by drawing up a list of responsibilities for one group of his employees. He worked hard on that list and then looked at it with a critical eye. "You know," he told us, "a list of job responsibilties is really nothing more than a job description."

We agreed wholeheartedly. That's exactly what it is—and a very useful job description indeed. Since it lists and defines the responsibilities of the job, it eliminates any discrepancy between what managers expect from their people and what the people *think* management expects. This list makes the job clear to everyone involved. Any differences in interpretation can be spotted at the beginning and cleared up in discussions between manager and employee.

Here is a set of guidelines that will help you set goals for your employees. You'll find these "rules" helpful every time you sit down to draw up a list of job responsibilities:

- Identify major areas of responsibility by title—"marketing," "sales," "service," "planning," and so on.
- Separate large areas of accountability, even though they may overlap somewhat. There may be no hard and fast boundaries between the various areas, but if you get too many activities under one key area heading, you'll find it hard to keep track of and evaluate your workers' performance.
- Group all related minor job responsibilities under one heading—for example, "completing a training program," "learning about new company policies and procedures," and "taking related university courses" could all come under the heading of "personal development." The number of activities in each area of responsibility should be roughly equal, if possible.
- Rank the responsibilties in order of importance. This order may shift after a time, so keep your plan flexible enough to accommodate any changes that occur.
- Limit your list to five or six major areas. Keep it simple.

Try making a list of your own job responsibilities as a manager. Then list the responsibilities of the people you supervise. Give as much thought and time as you can spare to making a really valid list. A good list will make the rest of your ROI planning—and the achievement of your ultimate goal — easier.

OBJECTIVES

You have now earned the *R* in ROI. Your next step is to break each responsibility down into the *O*—objectives.

An objective is a specific, measurable result to be achieved within a certain time. It tells you *what* you are to do, *how much* work you must accomplish, and *when* that work must be finished.

We asked Tim Stone to tell us about some current project he had listed as one of his own responsibilities in the area of planning.

"I've got a lulu," he told us. "It's all I've been able to think about for the past few weeks. We have a hot new product coming on the market in a few months, and my department has to come up with a user's manual to go with it."

"Good. Then you're in the planning stage right now," we said. "Why don't you set down your objectives for that planning?"

"You mean I should figure out exactly what my people and I have to do to get the project off the ground?"

"Yes. Identify each separate task you need to accomplish. How many separate tasks do you think there are?"

"I won't know until I start listing them, but they'll all have to be finished by—let's see—the end of next week if we want to have the user's manual ready when the product hits the stores."

"The end of next week is November 6th. That's your deadline, right?"

"Right."

"Okay, that's one planning objective: to identify all of the individual tasks you have to perform in order to finish the user's manual by November 6th."

Tim formulated an aim that fulfilled the basic requirements for a good objective:

- A good objective tells *what* you have to do—identify the tasks that have to be accomplished in order to get the job done on time.
- It tells *how much* or *how many* tasks you must perform—all of them.
- It tells *when*—by November 6th.

To be effective, an objective must clearly state the end result you desire, the amount of work you must do, and the specific time by which the work must be completed.

You might also want to add to your objective a qualifying phrase of some sort. It can be a means of measuring the success of your work, or it may be a helpful description of some sort. For example, instead of saying just "tasks," you might say "tasks that require preliminary actions."

Set objectives only for Key Result Areas (KRAs) if a responsibility is in a maintenance phase. The standard needs to be known. The idea is to keep the number of objectives to a manageable few—only the important ones. You need a number that is "do-able" without having to leap tall buildings in a single bound in order to accomplish everything.

Here are some guidelines that will help you develop objectives:

- Establish *what* you need to accomplish; decide *how much* of the work you must do or *how many* tasks must be completed ("all the tasks," "one project schedule," "16,000 names"); determine *when* you must finish the work ("every Thursday morning," "by November 6th," "in sixty days").
- Qualify the objective, if necessary, with a helpful description of a task, and additional means of measuring performance, or an explanation of how thoroughly the job needs to be done.
- Be specific. Here is a useful objective: "Decrease the number of repeat service calls due to service representatives' errors." Now, here is

an objective that is vague and meaningless: "Increase the quality of service."

- Make the objectives challlenging but attainable; they should be neither too easy nor too hard.
- Set objectives for each responsibility, even though you may not have complete control over everything involved in reaching them. You'll still get better results in the long run if you know where you want your employees—and yourself—to be at a certain time and if you have a plan for getting there, even though you may have to revise it as you go along.

INDICATORS

"This is really helpful stuff," Tim said, "especially that last guideline. The list will give me a framework to hang my own actions on. I guess we come now to the _I_ in ROI—the _indicators_. They show our progress, right? Could we call them milestones? They'll show me how far I've gone from where I started and how close I am to the place I'm trying to reach?"

"Right. Actually, 'milestones' is a terrific metaphor for 'indicators.' Like a milestone, an indicator is specific and measurable, a sign showing exactly how much progress a person has made toward his or her goal."

Indicators are actually mini-objectives, in a way. They mark the steps you must take to reach your objectives. Like objectives, they describe an action, specify an end result, and indicate the deadline for accomplishing that result.

Most people need help in putting a goal into small incremental steps even when they understand it. If indicators are simple, clear, and easy to accomplish, the objective will be reached.

A recent survey in the automobile industry showed that if a salesperson can discover the customer's needs and demonstrate the appropriate automobile, the person has a 50 percent chance of making a sale. In auto sales as well as industries like implements and computers—any business in which an actual hands-on experience can influence the customer's decision—the demonstration is the key component. The indicator then becomes "What do I need to do in order to be able to hold a demonstration?"

One enterprising dealer selling an expensive foreign car concentrated on the affluent market where the greatest sales potential lay. He called individuals in that market and offered them the use of a car on weekends. As had been predicted, he was able to sell cars to just about half of the people who accepted the offer.

A textile plant with fourteen locations in the Southeast was threatened by unionization. At the policymaking level, the top managers felt that they would be able to get a positive business message to the employees on the factory floor if their managers and supervisors could talk to individual workers several times a day; ideally five times a day. To this end, managers and supervisors were asked to keep a record of how often they spoke to each employee. Times ranged from one and one-half to just under three encounters a day. When the vote for union certification came, it was directly proportional to the amount of communication each plant had achieved. The company won through caring and communication, and through their tenacious tracking of the indicator.

Let's return to Tim's objective: to get the user's manual done by November 6th. On his way to that objective he might have to pass this milestone—or indicator: "Send a memo to each of the three department supervisors asking them to give us a list of the tasks their department has to accomplish in order to get the manual started. The memos must go out by Friday, October 30."

This indicator includes the three vital kinds of information:

- *What?* Send memos.
- *How much—or how many?* Three, one to each of three supervisors.
- *When?* By Friday, October 30.

Indicators allow employees to keep track of their own performance. The same indicators will show you whether or not your people are accomplishing their objectives. Indicators, in other words, provide an early warning system by showing whether an employee is on schedule, ahead of schedule, or behind it. They tell you whether you should speed things up or keep going at the same pace. They show you whether there's a lot of "fat"—extra time—in your schedule or whether it gives the employee just barely time enough to get the work done.

Here are the guidelines for establishing indicators:

- Have at least one indicator for each objective.
- Make the indicators specific and measurable. Like objectives, they should tell specifically *what* has to be done and *how much* work (or *how many* tasks) must be done.
- Create a time limit for each indicator in one of three ways: (1) by following an ongoing schedule ("one a month"); (2) by setting an ongoing but irregular schedule ("before each presentation"); or (3) by working on a one-time-only basis with a definite date ("by November 11").
- Be sure the indicators are directly related to the objectives. Remember Pareto's 20–80 rule? Your employees perform a great many

measurable tasks, but not all of them send you hurtling toward your objectives. The indicators should not only show you what your employees are doing but should also help you pick out the most productive tasks your people perform—the effective 20 percent.

- Make indicators easy to use. They must provide immediate and constant feedback. (We won't talk about feedback here; it is the subject of Chapter 7.) Your employees shouldn't have to waste their time trying to figure out what the indicators say.

THE CASE STUDY

"Okay," we said to Tim. "Now you've got all the guidelines; one set for Responsibilities, another set for Objectives, and a third set for Indicators—the complete ROI."

"They're a big help, that's for sure," Tim said. "It makes me really eager to start setting up a ROI system in my own section."

"It would be good practice for you to do a case study of one of your employees. Maybe choose an employee who's been having some performance problems."

"That gives me a lot of people to choose from!"

Case studies will prepare you for those times when everything is going up at once and you wonder where all your careful planning went. The information you get from a case study helps you keep a hold on things.

Make a case study of your own based on one of your own people by following these steps.

Your first step, of course, is to choose the employee who will be its subject. You'd do best, as we just said, to pick someone whose performance has been slipping lately. It should be an employee who has been with you long enough for you to get to know him or her quite well.

Once you've chosen the employee for your case study, you can move on to the next step: Go over your own list of responsibilities for that worker —the list you drew up when we were discussing the *R* in ROI, responsibilities. It's been quite some time since you wrote that list, so you'll have to spend some time checking it carefully. Examine every item on the list and then ask yourself two questions: Have I included the employee's most important responsibilities? Does my list include any task that is not actually this employee's responsibility?

When you're sure that the list gives an accurate picture of the person's job responsibilities, go on to the case study itself. Ask yourself some more questions: How well—or how poorly—does this worker handle the first responsibility on the list? Is it time to sit down with this employee and find out what's wrong? Once we've identified the problem, we can work together to make things right again.

Go on down the list of responsibilities doing the same thing. As you work, keep your mind on all three elements of the ROI system:

- Responsibilities
- Objectives
- Indicators

Once you have examined all of the employee's responsibilities, go back to the top of the list and do two more things:

1. Break each responsibility down into objectives.
2. Identify indicators for each objectives.

Indicators, remember, are your milestones. You will proceed from the first indicator to the second to the third, and so forth, until you reach your objective. As you go along, describe each specific task the employee must perform in order to reach the objective in question. Keep in mind that more than one kind of action will accomplish the same result. Be sure to find indicators that provide definite feedback (see Chapter 6), so that you can use them to monitor the employee's progress.

Make changes in and additions to your case study whenever the need arises. You'll probably discover that the case study is a valuable tool for helping the worker whose performance has been slipping. It assists you in determining what has gone wrong; from there you can go on to decide how to make things right again.

INDIVIDUAL CONFERENCES

When you're ready to put ROI into effect, you'll start by having conferences with each individual worker. Here are some tasks you might want to accomplish during those conferences:

- Agree on the responsibilities, objectives, and indicators of the employee's job. Be prepared to negotiate and, if necessary, to compromise. Employees know their own jobs very well, and they may have valid reasons for doing something one way when you think it should be done some other way. Just be sure ahead of time that you know what you will not give up and what you are willing to let go. That way, you'll have something to bargain with.
- Make the organization's goals very clear to the employee; once

that's done, you can negotiate realistic goals and objectives for each individual.

- Identify the areas where you're going to have to provide support for the employee. (You'll find that the discussion will automatically lead you to those areas.)
- Set up a schedule for reviewing the employee's ROI regularly.

If this seems like a great deal of trouble to go to, keep in mind that a truly successful work unit is worth all the effort it takes. Anyway, once you get used to positive management, you'll do all these things automatically.

Talking It Out

Linda is discussing her ROI with her manager, Tony. They have clarified the result areas for which she is accountable—her primary responsibilities. They are now about to discuss the other two elements of ROI: objectives and indicators.

TONY   Then you believe your primary objective right now is the new project, right?

LINDA   Yes. It seems to me that this project ought to have top priority for the moment. What do you think?

TONY   I agree. In your memo you indicated a project deadline of September first. Have you decided exactly what steps you will have accomplished by that date?

LINDA   That's the date on which the new design procedures will be implemented.

TONY   Yes, that's what you say in your memo, but let's see if we can make this more specific. What, exactly, do you mean by "implemented"? Do you mean you'll have the procedures in use by some or all or a few of the people in your section?

LINDA   Ah, now I see what you mean by "more specific." When I say that the procedures will be implemented by September first, I mean that each employee will have a full understanding of them. In other words, my department will be working at full capacity under the new system by September first. I guess I should reword that objective, Tony. Let's try this: The objective is to have the new design procedures in place and being capably and fully used by all of the people in my department by September first. How does that sound?

TONY   Good. Your original statement of objective was okay, too, but I think this one is better because it's more precise. Now let's talk about action steps. Suppose you tell me what you have in mind; then we'll exchange ideas on the subject.

LINDA   Yes, I'll want to hear your suggestions—especially in regard to possible time problems. Here's the thing, Tony. In order to have my staff working at full capacity by the first of September, I'll have to get them all trained by August first. Now we know from past experience that people need a full month of practice on a new procedure before they reach the point at which they can use it with ease. During that first month after training, they'll make mistakes; they'll have to stop often to look things up or ask questions; and they'll work more slowly than usual out of lack of confidence in their understanding of the system. But after one month of practice, they'll be right back at peak performance; the new procedures will be familiar to them and easy to use.

TONY   Okay, so all of your people must be fully trained by August first. Now, you mentioned a possible time problem. Do you think they'll need more than a month of practice on the new procedures?

LINDA   No. One month will be fine. The problem is that we'll have to train all of them during the last two weeks in July. That's the only time I can spare them long enough for them to complete the training course.

TONY   That's cutting it awfully close, isn't it?

LINDA   Yes, and we could run into problems. For example, we'll have people on vacation at that time, and we'll have to train them when they return in August. That will cut into the vital practice period.

TONY   Suppose we start training earlier? Can we schedule half of your people for instruction during the first two weeks of July and the other half during the last two weeks?

LINDA   That would be ideal, but I don't see how we can free any of the people in my department for training before the middle of the month. We have three big jobs to complete between July first and July fourteenth. If we schedule, say, half or even a third of my people for training during those first two weeks, we won't be able to complete those three jobs on time. So it looks as if we'll just have to cram all of the training into the last half of July, after those jobs are out of the way.

TONY   I know that one of the jobs is the Kensington system; that can't be put off. What about the other two?

LINDA   The Ricoh design and the Stebbins system.

TONY   Well, the Stebbins job has to go out on schedule, but let me see what I can do about Ricoh, Linda. I'm almost certain I can postpone that deadline for five or six weeks. If we can get your people out from under the Ricoh work, could we train half of them in early July and the rest during the last two weeks of the month?

LINDA   Yes. That way we could also make sure nobody misses training because of vacation time.

TONY   But you'll have to revise your action step, won't you?

LINDA   Yes. Let's see. Now the action step is to train half of my staff by July fifteenth and the other half by July thirty-first. I appreciate your help in rescheduling the Ricoh job. It'll be much better this way.

TONY   Okay. Now let's talk about indicators. How are you going to know if you've accomplished your objective of getting the new procedure implemented and in full use by September first?

LINDA   The trainers and I have devised a competency test—a series of tests, actually, of graduated difficulty. Using the results of these tests, I can make sure all of my people are working at an eighty percent competency level or better by September first. The earliest tests will be a part of the training, so we'll find out right away if somebody needs help or needs more practice in any area. We'll be able to give that person attention on the spot, retest him or her later on, and make sure the problems are all ironed out.

TONY   And during the practice period? The month of August, I mean. Have you devised any indicators to show that your people are progressing toward the goal of full implementation by September first?

LINDA   We'll give the last two parts of the competency test during August. And each person will keep a chart showing the amount of work he or she accomplishes each day. They do that under the system we're using now; the charts serve as work logs. When people get bogged down, they discuss the problem with me, and together we figure out a way to smooth things out. When we start the new system, they'll expect their logs to show a decline in production in the early days, with a gradual increase as they progress toward September. If they reach a certain level and get stuck there, then we'll try to figure out what's wrong and get them moving toward their previous production levels. By September first they should, in fact, be working above their old rates, because this new system is so much faster and more efficient than the old one.

TONY   Then the production charts should work well as indicators, provided you keep in close touch with your people. Well, I know you always keep in touch, but you'll probably want to make yourself more available than usual during the training and practice periods, right?

LINDA   Absolutely. They'll need plenty of help at first and tons of encouragement.

TONY   About this series of competency tests, Linda. You said you and the trainers developed it together?

LINDA   Yes. I think it's quite good. Each test in the series will determine the person's level of competency in certain areas. We'll get the people up to eighty percent in one area before moving them forward to another skill. The test will be printed up by tomorrow. If you like I'll have a copy on your desk by lunchtime. After you've had a chance to look it over, I'll welcome any suggestions.

TONY   Fine. Linda, I'm very pleased with the way you've handled this project. You went ahead and planned this whole thing step by step, considering all possible contingencies and making good use of the information you accumulated during past projects. Then, when I suggested a change in your schedule, you accepted it and adjusted to it without any sign of inflexibility.

LINDA   This ROI system works well for me, and it suits me, I think. It takes all of the vagueness out of my job, and it gives order to what used to seem like an unmanageable number of unrelated tasks. And I feel much less anxious about my job now. In the old days I might have tensed up if you'd suggested a big change in my training scheule, but now I can see that the instruction is not an end in itself but merely a means of accomplishing a goal, and it's the goal that I have to keep in mind every minute.

TONY   Good. Next time maybe we can talk about your feedback system. From what I've heard today, you seem to have an excellent one in operation already.

CHAPTER 7

I MUST BE DOING SOMETHING RIGHT: MANAGING THROUGH THE INFLUENCE OF FEEDBACK

"Accentuate the positive,
Eliminate the negative..."
    —*Popular song of the 1940s*
"How'm I doin'?"
    —*New York City Mayor Edward Koch*

"**H**OW'M I DOING" IS THE QUESTION CALLED UP BY the next segment of your management wheel, effective management through *feedback*. But many people, like Mayor Koch, expect people to answer that question with a value judgment: "You're doing fine!" "You're doing okay," or even "You're not doing too well." Good feedback, however, is free of value judgment. It's like the dial on the scale that tells you how much you weigh—*not* whether it's good or bad to weigh that much. It's like the gas gauge on your car that tells you how much fuel you have in your tank—not that you've been careless to let your gas level get so low, or that you showed commendable foresight to fill the tank when you did. Those are judgments that you—and sometimes others—make on the basis of the information you've gotten from feedback.

Good feedback is free of value judgments.

On-the-job feedback should be like a gas gauge—completely nonjudgmental. Why? Because feedback that implies a value judgment—"You're doing great!" or "You're a professional disaster area!"—will not get your employees to improve their performance one whit. Feedback that erroneously leads people to believe they're doing great, in fact, is likely to get you into heavy trouble. Suppose your people find that they have successfully met a certain indicator (in other words, suppose the feedback says, "You're doing great!"). They'll expect a reward of some sort, won't they? At the very least, they'll expect you to pat them on the back and tell them how wonderful they are. Then, when you don't come through with the expected praise they'll be (1) hurt, (2) confused, (3) resentful, (4) unlikely to knock themselves out for you in the future. . . and so forth, ad infinitum.

What if things go the other way—which is more likely—and the feedback provides a negative value judgment ("You're just lazy!")? Well, that will put you in even deeper trouble. Any one or all of the following sticky situations could result:

- By giving your workers only negative feedback, you'll cast yourself as the bearer of bad news, the kind of manager whose employees expect criticism every time the manager approaches them.
- Negative feedback robs your people of the very responsibility you should be transferring over to them. It says, "Look, I tried to give you some responsibility, and you couldn't handle it." To which many people will be tempted to reply, "Next time do it yourself." Not a nice situation for anyone involved.
- Employees who crave attention are inclined to use negative feedback as a means of getting you to notice them and spend time with them.

("Could you please explain to me *exactly* what I'm doing wrong?")
Keep in mind that many people would rather face criticism—and
even abuse—than get no attention at all. Sad as that sounds, it's
true; ask any teacher in school.

* A value judgment has no corrective force; it won't lead to a change
  for the better.

"But," protested our manager friend, Tim Stone, "it's important to
let your people know when they're doing something wrong."

"It is, sure. It's also important—and a lot of managers forget this—to
let them know they're doing something *right*!"

Tim grinned. "I know. I have to keep reminding myself to do that."

"It's something we all have to remind ourselves to do, Tim. You're talking about the pat on the back or the slap on the wrist. That's *reinforcement*,
and we will talk about it later. But right now we're concerned with *feedback*."

THE EMERY EXAMPLE

Feedback is vital to good performance. In fact, it is just as important as
praising an employee for doing a good job, or insisting on an improved performance. Perhaps even more important, because it's only through feedback that you can really know what kind of job someone is doing. Tim
Stone gave us an example of the experience of one company—Emery Air
Freight.

Emery's policy was to urge their dock supervisors and warehouse people to consolidate a number of small packages for the same destination into
one large container. Clearly, the practice saved money; in fact, the saving
was so significant that management periodically asked the dock managers
to estimate how often the containers were used. The estimate was almost always the same—about 90 percent of the time.

Emery vice-president Edward Feeney decided to check that estimate by
actual observation. Much to his surprise, he found that the containers were
being used only 45 percent of the time—half of what the dock managers
had estimated.

We asked Tim Stone what he thought Feeney might have done when he
discovered this discrepancy.

"Well, back in the old days," Tim said, "he would've fired the dock
managers. He'd have decided that either they were lying to him or they
weren't up on what was happening in their department. But things are different now, so I don't know *what* he would've done."

We told Tim that Feeney didn't even consider firing the dock managers. He knew they weren't being dishonest. Feeney realized that they weren't getting any feedback on how often the containers were actually being used. And because they didn't *know* what was happening, they based their estimates on what they *thought* was happening.

When the company provided feedback—and that turned out to be a very easy thing to do—the results were amazing. The company proved very conclusively that the employees really liked the idea of consolidating small shipments into large containers. They simply hadn't realized how seldom they were doing it.

Here's how Feeney and his people turned the situation around. To show the dock managers how often containers were really used, Emery provided each dockworker with a checklist. Each time the employee used a container, he checked the list. In a single day, the use of containers jumped 95 percent! The employees and managers could actually see, for the first time, what they were really doing. Emery saved $250,000 during the first year it used this new system of warehouse feedback.

Notice: The feedback was neutral—nonjudgmental. It consisted of checkmarks on a list. Nobody said, "You're doing great" or "You're doing terrible." The lists simply told the employees how often they used the containers—not whether their actions were good or bad. Often, however, workers *perceive* feedback as a comment on their performance. Even at Emery, a worker who checked only two containers out of a possible twenty would be bound to think, "Gosh, I'm not doing so well." And anyone who had numerous checkmarks would be encouraged to see those spaces fill up and would say, "Wow! I'm doing a terrific job." But the list itself is simply a marker.

Most employees want to perform well, but if they have no feedback, they can't measure their performance. At Emery, the workers were given feedback; their checklists told them whether they were using the containers often or seldom.

FINDING FEEDBACK DATA

No matter what the work situation, feedback is there; it just hasn't been identified and passed on to the people who can make the most productive use of it. One of your jobs as a manager is to be sure that all available information is being used. Finding and using the feedback will provide a reward for you as well as for your workers. Here's how: If the feedback shows that your people are reaching or coming close to their goals, they'll keep on doing whatever they're doing. And you, of course, have tied those

goals in to the company's mission, so *you're* getting benefits, too.
Feedback comes from a variety of sources:

- the manager
- other employees
- the job itself
- a company appraisal system
- the employee's own observations and perceptions

A survey has found that the most useful kind of feedback comes either from the employees themselves or from their supervisor.

GUIDELINES FOR PROVIDING FEEDBACK

- *Keep the feedback neutral.* It shouldn't praise; it shouldn't blame; *it should inform.* Period. In his book, *Trust,* Dr. Jake Gibbs identifies feedback as negative when it has one or more of these six characteristics:

  1. judgment
  2. superiority
  3. certainty
  4. control
  5. manipulation
  6. indifference

- *Provide feedback as soon as possible.* The quicker you and the employees see and can interpret the feedback, the sooner you can make adjustments and get better results. There's also another reason for providing fast feedback. How would you feel if you did what you *hoped* was a good job but didn't really *know* for three or four weeks? How would you feel if you did your work without being aware that a misstep early in the job was leading to useless work that you would have to do over several weeks later?

- *Don't try to give feedback on every single task leading to an objective.* Pick out the tasks that are not going too well, and devise feedback for them. But be careful to keep the information neutral: "Five new accounts in April; six new accounts in May; four new accounts in June"—*not* "Oops! What happened in June? Little slip-up there!"

- *Provide feedback frequently.* You and the employee need to know that a previous adjustment put things back on the right track, or that further changes are needed.

- *Use information that relates to your employees' goals.* When you set up your ROI program, you were made aware that each of the objectives has indicators. The feedback should directly reflect whether the employee has successfully met each indicator; this gives a concrete measure of progress toward the objective.

Let's take as an example an insurance agent whose objective is to generate names and qualifying information for 1,500 prospects over the coming year. Sixty percent of these prospects are to be referrals. Each week, the agent can see that if he comes close to thirty prospects, and about eighteen of them are referrals, he is doing what he should. Those are his indicators—thirty prospects, eighteen referrals a week. The necessary feedback could be provided by a simple chart:

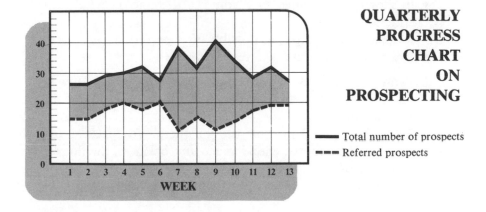

QUARTERLY
PROGRESS
CHART
ON
PROSPECTING

—— Total number of prospects
--- Referred prospects

Here you can see that graphic feedback (charts, diagrams, tables, and so forth) will sometimes be more effective than words. For this agent, graphing is not the only easiest way to keep an eye on things, but the clearest as well. You can see that the agent *was* averaging thirty prospects a week or better; the top line on the graph stays between twenty-eight and forty—more often on the high side of thirty than below it.

The graph makes something else clear. Note how the dotted line dips during the weeks when the solid line soars. At week 8, the *solid* line dips a bit while the dotted line rises. This shows the agent something he might not have been aware of without the graph: When he was pushing too hard to have a *lot* of prospects every week, he didn't get such *good* ones. In this objective, quality is really more important than quantity, so this feedback shows the agent a practical way to improve his performance—by spending time and effort getting referred prospects.

As we said earlier, studies have found that the best feedback comes directly from the employee and is monitored by you, the manager. It allows the employee to take responsibility for the results, and the manager to check on the progress of the work.

REQUIREMENTS FOR GOOD FEEDBACK

- It lets both you and the employee know when problems are developing and where.
- Interpreting takes very little of the employee's time and almost none of your own.
- It does not require anyone to fill in complicated forms or a bothersome amount of extra paperwork.
- It shows your people that you are there to provide help, *not* criticism.
- It appears as promptly as possible after performance.
- It is accurate, concise, and readily usable.

Do you give feedback to your employees? How often? How do you give it—in meetings? in individual discussions? on paper? How do your employees react to it?

"You know," said Tim, "off the job there's feedback all over the place—stock market reports, checking account balances, the floor indicators that light up as an elevator goes up or down . . ."

"And the car speedometer, the thermometer outside your kitchen window . . ."

"The cost-of-living index!" Tim finished triumphantly. "How come these seem to be used everyplace but at work?"

"That's one of the things we're aiming to change," we said.

Tim was thoughtful. "My people sure don't like anything that smacks of performance charts. That's not an effective kind of feedback, I guess."

"Almost nobody likes them, Tim. But you'll find that your people will really appreciate feedback if you introduce it right and keep it *fair and neutral*. One good way to do that is to use charts or graphs. How would you persuade one of your employees to graph his or her own performance? You might point out the benefits of graphic feedback. Later on, you might reinforce the employee in some way for giving it a try.

Charts and graphs have several advantages as vehicles for feedback:

- They give concrete, visual meaning to abstract concepts like "improvement," "lack of improvement," and "stable performance."

At one glance, you see a performance history in concrete units of measurement.

- Information from them is easy to communicate.
- You and your employees can quickly refer to them as often as necessary.
- They are good tools for planning the remainder of the task, and they can help you plan similar projects in the future.
- They allow you to distinguish between short-term and long-term progress.
- The manager can use the chart or graph as a basis for giving rewards; the chart lets the employee anticipate the reward.

"You've worked out some ROI goal-setting plans for your people," we said to Tim Stone. "How about setting up a chart for one of them, to provide feedback on the progress of the project?"

"How about pointing me in the right direction?"

"Sure. First, figure out exactly which results or action steps you want to measure. Then set this up in a two-dimensional pattern, with the quantity or frequency or whatever along the vertical axis, and time along the horizontal. What do you want to use as an example, Tim?"

He thought for a moment. "Our market research people have been doing a big survey, testing the market for five different new products we're planning to introduce nationwide. They've got thousands of filled-in questionnaires. Of course, we put all the answers on the computer, and that's where we're having some trouble.

"The keyboarder I've got doing it has shown herself to be very good on some other jobs, but she seems to be falling down here. It's been a terrific bottleneck. I honestly don't know if the problem is that the employee is slow or just that the material is unusually difficult to handle."

"What if you had a chart showing the number of questionnaires she can input per—per what?"

"Per hour."

"That way you'd get a look at the pattern over time and your employee would be able to see the picture as well. Would that be any help to you?"

"Yes, it would. If I find we can't come reasonably near the rate we ought to have, I'll have to put someone on nights to do the extra computer work. But if I see that the keyboarder who's doing it now does well some of the time—as well as she's done on previous jobs—but not consistently, I'll suspect the problem is with her."

"So there's a double advantage to keeping this chart. If you suspect the employee is having some kind of problem with her work, you'll be in a position to straighten her out. Okay, let's label the vertical axis 'Average Questionnaires Input per Hour,' and figure the average at the end of each day. What should the range be?''

"I'd say between eighteen and forty-five. She's not doing any better than an average of twenty now, at the most. And if she could get up to forty-five, we'd be home free.''

"Well, let's put in a few more at the top, just as a margin. Okay, now we need some kind of baseline from which to go onward and upward. You say she's doing an average of about twenty an hour?''

"That's what I think.''

"That's close enough. We'll make day one the day you started inputting the information. Has she stepped up her rate any since you started?''

"We've only been on it about four weeks,'' Tim said, shuffling through the papers on his desk. "I've got the figures here—'' It took him a little while to extract the answer from the papers in front of him. He sounded surprised as he said, "Gee, it looks like she's stayed at about the same level.''

"When you start charting it, you'll be able to see that kind of thing right away, while it's happening,'' we said.

We put in the baseline for the first four weeks—a dotted line just below 20 on the vertical scale—and plotted the actual performance around it.

"Now, what do you think a realistic goal would be?''

Tim shrugged. "I'd hoped she could do nearly forty-five, but I don't know how realistic that is.''

"Give it a try. When you see how hard it is for the keyboarder to get her average up, you can decide whether you'll have to put another keyboarder on the night shift.''

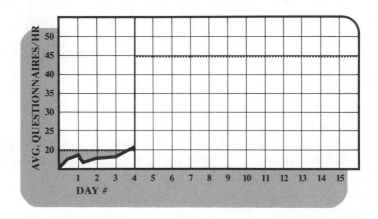

"There you have it, Tim. Let your employee herself put in her average per hour.''

It's important that the feedback system "belong" to the employee—not to the manager. That way, it's not a "report card" that the manager is holding over the employee's head; it is the person's own guide to performance, which remains the employee's own responsibility.

"Your keyboarder can mark the chart, but it's important that you discuss it with her periodically. If she just uses it to keep track of her performance, the activity could turn into nothing more than a kind of record-keeping. The information itself is valuable, but it's not enough *in* itself. You've got to create an atmosphere where it seems natural to share information—to talk about it. This employee is going to need help from you, too—and a lot of encouragement—if she's going to move up from twenty questionnaires an hour to forty-five."

"I know, and I'm prepared to give it to her. She's a good worker. I have confidence that if anybody can do it, she can. But this is a more complex survey than any we've done before, and it just may be that the keyboarding has to take a lot longer. We'll see."

"You will now, if you use the graph."

One of the best reasons for give and take between the employee and the manager about feedback is that it offers the manager a chance to reinforce any good news that the feedback shows and also to deal with the bad news in such a way that it isn't presented negatively. Don't present it as some kind of punishment, but as information about a problem that needs to be dealt with, that employee and manager can tackle together.

We're going to go into this matter of reinforcement in detail in a later chapter. Right now it's important to point out that feedback itself can be reinforcing. When employees know that they are making progress toward their goals, the knowledge can be enough of a stimulus for them to continue to improve their performance.

Managers who don't use feedback find themselves reacting rather than leading—putting out fires that feedback could have prevented. Even though employees are using self-feedback *and* are communicating with the manager about what their charts or graphs reveal, still other areas have to be covered. (There is performance that cannot be broken down into action steps. Feedback for that kind of performance must come directly from the manager.) But because their jobs involve so many urgent responsibilities, some managers feel they can't find time to give personal feedback.

"I like the idea of employees 'owning' their feedback," Tim told us. "*I* don't have time to do much about it myself; it seems as if we managers get more responsibilities all the time..."

"We know that," we told him. "That's why we've worked out a method we call the Two-to-Four-Minute Feedback Session."

"If it's really two to four minutes, I could fit it in," Tim said. "I can find that much time to give to every one of my people each week. But how much could you accomplish in that short a time?"

"You'd be surprised. And it really takes only two to four minutes. Five simple steps, that's all."

THE TWO-TO-FOUR-MINUTE FEEDBACK SESSION

Step One

Begin by praising the employee for one thing he or she did well in one specific part of the job—one outstanding success. Be brief and be *positive*.

JON:	Thanks for this report, Laura.
LAURA:	You've read it?
JON:	Four times.
LAURA:	Four times! Does that mean it's confusing?
JON:	Laura, it's terrific. I read it four times because there's so much meat in it.
LAURA:	Whew! I was a little worried about it. I didn't pull any punches.
JON:	I noticed that. But you socked it to me in the right way; you were constructive about it. I realize now that I haven't made myself clear sometimes when clarity was critical, and that had an adverse effect on the work we turned out.
	You made me see, too, that we've been focusing our cost-cutting on short-term things that don't really save any money in the long run. We *should* have been working harder to create an environment where people want to do their best. You've said all this well, and you've said it objectively. I admire this report a lot.
LAURA:	Well, thanks. That's a load off my mind.

Step Two

Ask the employee's opinion about the work. "How do you think you did?" This gives the person a chance to express some feelings, even blow off steam, if necessary.

JON: How do you feel about this, Laura?

LAURA: I'm proud of it. I was kind of worried about how you'd take it; it *is* critical of you, in some ways. But all in all, I think I did a good job.

Step Three

Ask the person, "What did you like best about what you did?" Follow that up by asking, "What else did you like?" Get at least three positive responses from the person. Ignore any negative comments. This will make your employees think *positively* about themselves and their work.

JON: What do you think is the best thing about your report?

LAURA: Well, I guess the way I presented the findings. I studied those figures very carefully, and I gave a lot of thought to the way I summarized them. I think it worked.

JON: Right. What else?

LAURA: What else? Oh, being able to come up with actual figures showing that working in a poor environment costs money. Statistics are a lot more convincing than general statements.

JON: And?

LAURA: I'm not sure I can put my finger on any other specific thing.

JON: Think about it. It doesn't have to be something in the report; it could be something about the job itself.

LAURA: I do like what I'm doing. I like the challenge of it.

JON: Okay!

Step Four

Then ask what one thing the employee will do differently next time.

JON: Tell me this, Laura. Is there anything you'd do differently next time?

LAURA: Yes, more than one. For instance, next time I'll point out the good things as well as the bad, so that people have a clear idea of what they're doing right.

Step Five

Summarize the session by repeating the three positive responses that the employee described to you, reassuring the employee and ending the session.

JON: Okay, Laura, this is the kind of report I hoped I'd get when I hired you. In fact, it's even better, because it's fair and objective and doesn't sidestep any problems. You've been able to back up all your findings, you've given me figures as well as theories, and I'm really glad to hear that you like your job.

"Hey!" Tim said. "Step Four is great! You turned something she did wrong into a positive statement. Her report was too negative, but instead of criticizing her for that, you let her point it out herself. That way, you made it constructive instead of negative."

"Exactly. That's important. Keep bad news from sounding negative; make it constructive. This focuses on the future instead of the past."

The value of the Two-to-Four-Minute Feedback Session is that it emphasizes the positive and lets the employee know how he or she is doing in the light of the job goal. As a result, it strengthens positive behavior, breaks up negative patterns, and encourages the employee to take responsibility for doing a better job.

"What if I ask 'How did it go?' in that second step and the guy just shrugs and says, 'I dunno!'" Tim asked.

"Then you'll just have to dig a little deeper. Sooner or later you'll get either a positive response, in which which case you go on to step three, or a negative one."

"And if it's negative?"

"That's not necessarily bad. At least your employee will get a gripe off his chest. That will give you a chance to find out that there *is* a problem and to tell the employee that you know it and that you're going to try to find a solution even if you haven't got one at your fingertips. When the person says something negative, listen. Pay attention, but don't dwell on it. With negative statements, and neutral ones, acknowledge what is said and then move on."

"Okay," said Tim. "I'm going to give it a try. I think this feedback stuff is very important, and there hasn't been nearly enough of it. What comes next? We've covered more than half of that management wheel."

"Well, we've been talking about reinforcement, so it's only fitting that the next thing we take up is the section of the wheel that has to do with rewards."

Talking It Out

Adam, a manager at a large manufacturing company, is conducting a Two-to-Four-Minute Feedback Session with Phil, a new employee.

ADAM   Phil, I just got a look at the figures for the past four weeks, and it appears that you people are doing a fine job of filling the orders. The charts show a steep drop in returns and complaints. I want you to know how much I appreciate your good work.

PHIL   Thanks, Adam. It gets crazy down here every now and then, but we do our best.

ADAM   And how about you, Phil? Are you beginning to feel at home on the job?

PHIL   Most of the time I feel as if I have things under control, except for the Henway account. I had some trouble on that one yesterday.

ADAM   What happened?

PHIL   Well, I sent them the right components but the wrong replenisher kits. They're not going to be thrilled about that.

ADAM   Maybe not, but it sounds as if you did a whole lot right and just one small thing wrong. You gave them the right components, didn't you? So that part of the order was fine. Remember, Phil, the Henway order is always a tough one to fill. Stand back for a moment, away from the one mistake you made, and take a look at the job as a whole. Forget about what yóu did wrong and tell me about the things you did right.

PHIL   Okay, let's see, now. I sent the right combinations of paper and cartridges. I never have trouble matching those up correctly.

ADAM   That's true. You don't make mistakes in that area. Now, what else did you do right?

PHIL   I got the whole rest of the order right, except for the replenisher kits, that is. I know all of Henway's needs now, and I know their materials. For instance, I can tell which rolls go with which machines even when the rolls aren't marked.

ADAM   And that's an extremely important skill, because very often the rolls come through unmarked. I think you understand Henway's product line very thoroughly. Now, what else are you good at?

PHIL   I'm fast. I feel very confident of my speed. I can put an order together quickly, even a big one like Simston's.

ADAM   I know you can, and believe me, we appreciate that. Now, Phil, what one thing will you do differently the next time you fill the Henway order?

PHIL   I've got to send the right replenisher kits next time. I suppose I'll have to memorize the stock so I can put the replenishers with the right materials.

ADAM   That'd be an awful lot of memorizing, Phil. Isn't there an easier way to solve this problem?

PHIL   Seems to me there's a chart somewhere that you can check to make sure things match up. It's color coded and it lets you check your kits against the other materials.

ADAM   The C-Five Chart?

PHIL   Yes. I guess that's what it's called. To tell you the truth I never realized I could be using that thing, but now that I think about it, I probably could have avoided the Henway mistake if I'd checked the chart before I sent out the order. I suppose I was thinking too much about speed; I figured it would take me an extra few minutes to pick up the C-Five Chart and cross-check the supplies. From now on, though, I'll worry a little bit less about my speed and a lot more about the accuracy of my orders. I'll still work as fast as I can, of course, but I'll check the C-Five often.

ADAM   That should solve your one little problem, then, Phil. Everything else was in fine shape, so it'll be worth a few extra minutes to get those combinations right. Anyway, I want you to know how much I appreciate your ability to get the paper and cartridge orders right, as well as your speed and your understanding of Henway's needs. You've been here only a short time, but you've already become a very valuable employee. Keep up the good work, Phil.

PHIL   Right. And from now on I'll make good use of the C-Five Chart.

CHAPTER 8

REWARDS: MANAGING THROUGH THE INFLUENCE OF REWARDS

"You want my vote? Sure, I know I owe my county job to you. I remember you got my brother Zeke out of jail last month. I ain't forgot it was you who fixed it so I don't have to pay any back taxes on the pasture land I own. But listen, Seth—what have you done for me lately?"

—Rural voter to candidate

"**H**OW IS IT," ASKED TIM STONE, "THAT WE'RE only now talking about rewards? Isn't that the first thing people think about when they're applying for a job—how much they're going to be paid, what kind of benefits there are, and all that? Seems to me we should've been talking about rewards at the very beginning."

"From the employee's point of view, yes, compensation—rewards—would be one of the first considerations. That's partly because it's hard to know much else about a job before you're actually in it. But this whole project you're engaged in with us, Tim—learning how to be a more effective and positive manager—means that you're dealing with people who are already in a job. So we're talking about rewards on the job. Answer this: How much control do you have over the salaries and fringe benefits of the people you supervise?"

"Hardly any," he answered. "Salaries and raises and fringe benefits—all the money issues—are controlled by our contract with the union, and by the company's salary schedules, and by seniority and by a dozen other things I can't do anything about. If I do want to get a raise or bonus for one of my people, I have to go way over my level, and sometimes it takes months for it to go through. *If* it goes through at all. So it looks as if I really don't have much to say about how my people are rewarded. So if that's the way it is, why are we even talking about rewards?"

"Tim, you can say—and do—a lot about how your people are rewarded. Listen to the experience a company much like yours had recently, and you'll understand better why we lay the subject of rewards on a manager like you."

TANGIBLE VS. INTANGIBLE REWARDS

We told Tim about a big company, with an accounting department of about seventy employees. Some time ago, top management found that work was coming out of the department with an alarming number of errors, and got pretty upset about it.

What to do? Somebody suggested that the managers explain the problem to the whole department, so they had a meeting—supervisors and employees together. They set some goals for better accuracy rates, and decided to post all the figures relating to the percentage of errors in their reports. They began charting their progress toward those goals. In other words, they gave the people in the accounting department the kind of graphic feedback we talked about in the previous chapter. In addition, every time a report had fewer errors than the norm that had been established, the managers praised the employee who had done the report. The results were excellent. In the accounts payable section, for instance, the error rate went from more than 8 percent to less than 0.2 percent! A hell of a good result! And it happened mainly because management handed out some pats on the back.

"True, other factors were tied in," we admitted. "In fact, the managers used every element of the management wheel. They gave the accountants a goal connected to the company's mission; they gave the employees full support; and they provided meaningful feedback by posting the figures. But the key reason for success in this instance is that the managers praised the employees every time they showed improvement."

"It's hard for me to imagine the employees considering praise all that valuable," Tim said. "Those people didn't get money or privileges or benefits—or any tangible rewards at all. Now I know people want to be told when they do a good job, but I find it a bit hard to believe they'd knock themselves out like that for a few kind words and nothing else!"

"Those few kind words meant a lot to the people who got them, Tim. It gave them real proof that what they were doing made sense—that their work had value and meaning. We all need to feel that what we do is worthwhile. That's why praise can sometimes be more effective than a raise in pay."

In a Japanese heavy industry plant, a chart is kept in each work unit showing the number of suggestions the employees contribute. Every suggestion is worth the equivalent of twenty-five yen, about ten cents, to the employee, regardless of its value, its length, or from whom it came. Those that are used earn higher rewards. The workers in every department get feedback on the number of suggestions they make. The company values the suggestions for their quantity alone, and finds that the quality has improved over time. Since this program was put into effect five years ago, the average worker has supplied about forty suggestions a year.

In the past, tangible rewards were more important than they are now. If the pay and fringe benefits were right, employees would put up with a great deal. But no more! A study made recently by *Psychology Today* magazine shows that that is no longer true. Employees of several companies were asked to rank eighteen different items connected with their jobs in what they saw as the order of their importance. The results? These intangible rewards led the list: (1) the chance to do something that makes you feel good about yourself; (2) the opportunity to accomplish something worthwhile; and (3) the chance to learn new things. Pay was way down in twelfth place, fringe benefits in sixteenth, and physical working conditions at rock-bottom, eighteenth place.

The survey went on to ask people how satisfied or dissatisfied they were with certain rewards in their own jobs. The researchers found the most dissatisfaction with rewards that had ranked near the bottom of the list in importance. New office furniture, for instance, isn't perceived as a thrilling reward.

Employees were most dissatisfied by not being allowed to participate in discussions about goals, by the lack of praise, by low pay and inadequate feedback, and by slim chances for promotion. All of this translates into deficiencies in three areas that should be familiar to us by now: goals, feedback, and rewards.

Intangible rewards lead to satisfied workers.

Any job offers two very different kinds of reward—tangible and intangible—and employees look for a satisfactory mix of the two. Before taking a job with a company, they ask practical questions: What does it pay? Will the company pick up all the medical insurance premium, or must I contribute? How much vacation will I get after I've worked for half a year? How long will it be before I'm up for a raise? How fast can I move up? Of course, the nature of the job is a consideration, too; people have frequently been known to take somewhat lower pay and fewer benefits if the work promises to be particularly interesting or challenging or especially well suited to them. But by and large it is the tangible rewards that make a person decide to come to work for this company instead of that one: the cash compensation (salary, bonuses), the benefits (insurance, pensions) and the perks (an office with a window, the use of a company car, seats in the firm's box at the ball game).

The intangible rewards are not always apparent to employees just starting out with a company; only after living with the job for a while do workers perceive those rewards—or the lack of them. But it is exactly this kind of reward that managers should be most concerned with. Managers, after all, control these rewards almost absolutely. When used right, they can be one of the managers' most valuable tools. These intangible, "social" rewards can make every difference in an employee's attitude toward the job.

The praise that made such a big difference to the accounting department's error rate is an intangible benefit. Here are some other intangible rewards that you can offer to your people:

- Give the employee some special individual attention.
- Send a memo congratulating someone for work well done.
- Pat one of your people on the back—literally!—and say, "Great job!"
- Give your people a chance to function more naturally and independently in their current jobs.
- Let someone take on a new responsibility.

- Ask an employee for his or her advice.
- Invite a worker to sit in on a meeting about a project in which he or she is involved.
- Let your people know that they are valuable to the company: "It was your shipping schedule that got these I-beams out on time, Jerry. We couldn't have made that deadline without you."
- Tell your employees that they are valuable to *you*: "I don't know what I'd have done without your understanding of that damned generator, Mike."

These intangible benefits—and the many others you'll devise to suit your own work situation—can make all the difference between an unsatisfied, inefficient employee and a worker who plunges enthusiastically into the job.

Of course your employees want a good salary, generous vacation times, company-financed medical plan, bonuses—all the financial rewards that are appropriate to the job. But they need the intangibles just as much. Dr. Frederick Herzberg has clearly explained why such a seemingly little thing as a few words of praise or appreciation can make such a big difference in the performance of an employee.

Dr. Herzberg distinguishes between tangible and intangible benefits in terms of two principles: the Hygiene Principle and the Motivation Principle. "Hygiene factors," he says, relieve physical discomforts such as hunger, thirst, cold, heat, and dampness. Thus hygiene factors *prevent dissatisfaction*.

Herzberg's Motivation Principle, on the other hand, involves "motivation factors," which *provide satisfaction*. Satisfaction comes from psychological growth, and that growth arises from the activities we perform. The more meaningful and challenging these activities are, the more satisfaction they provide.

"Do you want to know the most significant part of this theory for a manager?" we asked Tim. "The dissatisfaction that the hygiene (tangible) factors can prevent, and the satisfaction that the motivator (or intangible) factors can engender *are not opposites*. The opposite of dissatisfaction is *no* dissatisfaction, and the opposite of satisfaction is *no* satisfaction.

In other words, tangible rewards—salary, benefits, and the like—do not provide satisfaction; they merely prevent dissatisfaction. And good performance can hardly be expected from employees whose only motivation is that they are not dissatisfied.

In contrast, Herzberg claims that intangible rewards—praise, responsibility, and so forth, in a job can provide the employee with satisfaction.

And good performance comes from satisfaction. Obviously, both kinds of needs must be met.

Ideally, there should be no dissatisfaction with the tangible rewards, and satisfaction with the intangible ones.

"The employer's task," says Herzberg, "is not to motivate his people to get them to achieve; he should provide opportunities for people to achieve so they will become motivated." There's an echo in that of something we said earlier in this book: You cannot make your employees love their jobs, but you can make the jobs more lovable. Motivation doesn't come from fringe benefits or good working conditions, higher wages, or status symbols. It does come from the successful achievement of a challenging task that fulfills the urge every one of us has to create something worthwhile.

"That statement," said Tim, "makes me feel very good. And optimistic."

"Why so?"

"Because those intangibles are exactly what I can give out whenever I think somebody's earned them, or needs them. I can't go to up to one of my people and say, 'You did a great job, so I'm going to get you a raise.' But I *can* say, 'You did a great job.' I just have to remember not to take people and their work for granted. If I stop to think how much that pat on the back meant to me when I began my career, I'll remember to give the same attention to the people I supervise. That's something I can do right away, whenever it's called for. *I* control that, and I like hearing that what I control is important."

REINFORCEMENT

Giving rewards to employees is known as *reinforcement*. We use this word because rewards strengthen—or reinforce—good behavior. In other words, an employee who gets a reward—or *reinforcer*—for doing a certain task well is likely to try hard to do it well again and again.

However, reinforcement has to be done correctly if it's going to be effective. Keep in mind the following characteristics of good reinforcement:

Rewards should be immediate, rather than delayed. It's not very encouraging to get thanks, no matter how lavish, four weeks after you've done someone a favor.

Each reinforcer should be individual and personal. Tailor the praise to the person and task you wish to reinforce. Telling the executive assistant to the president that her typing is very neat is patronizing and could be interpreted as an insult, like telling a neurosurgeon that she ties her surgical mask on well. The assistant's sophisticated understanding of company policy is unique to her; her typing is simply a basic-skill that she takes for granted. A new employee fresh out of business school and nervous in the typing pool, however, might regard the same comment as significant praise indeed. Here is a more effective compliment to the executive assistant: "You seem to know exactly how much detail to contribute after the boss has made his general statement, and how much to omit. If you're asked for more information, you can always provide it. I don't know how you do it. You're terrific."

Reinforcement for doing something is more effective than a reward for not doing something.

An accountant might cringe to hear you say, "I'm real glad you didn't make any errors in calculation in the Fairwell Trucking account," because you're praising him for something he *didn't* do wrong. The same accountant, however, would probably be delighted to have you say, "You're doing an excellent job on the Fairwell account. They're real pleased, and so am I." Now you're rewarding him for something he *did* do right.

Make your comments positive, not negative. Don't tell the machine shop to turn out fewer bad parts; tell them it'd be great if their percentage of good parts went up. That happened in a real shop. At first, the manager posted charts that showed the percentage of rejects. There was some improvement, but not much. After a while, he withdrew the charts. Later, he put up new charts, recording the percentage of parts that had passed inspection. Lo and behold, the number of good parts increased dramatically. Just the turnaround from negative to positive reinforcement triggered an improvement.

Try intangible reinforcers before turning to tangible ones.

People can never receive too much praise. The more intangible support you give them, the more satisfied they are likely to be.

"A good manager is always on the lookout for opportunities to provide positive reinforcement," we told Tim. "Even in a terrible situation, you should be able to find something to praise. In fact, positive reinforcement is crucial when things are going badly. Look at the situation carefully. Pick out the things that are going wrong, and shove them aside. Now find one task that's being done well. And *praise* your people for doing it. In other words, come up with some valuable reinforcer instead of doling out criticism."

"How about giving me some examples of good reinforcement?" Tim asked.

"Tell you what. We'll set up some typical situations and show you two different managers' responses to them. You tell us which manager provides the positive reinforcement."

Here are the examples we gave Tim. The difference in response is not hard to spot!

1. *Employee:* Why does this customer have to wait two weeks for delivery?

   Manager A: I answered that question two weeks ago!

   Manager B: I'm glad you feel free to ask questions. The delay results from a technical weakness. We've tried—and we're still trying—to speed up the customization process, but until someone develops a faster-drying enamel, we'll have to live with the two-week wait.

2. *Employee:* I don't see any reason for adding up all these entries. We never do anything with the totals.

   Manager A: Well, somebody must want them or we wouldn't be asked to do them.

   Manager B: That's a good question. That kind of thinking is a sure sign you've going to really get ahead here. Why don't you give the standards department a ring and ask them if they have a reason for telling you to add up the entries?

3. *Employee:* Could you please look over my report and tell me if I'm on the right track?

   Manager A: No, no, no! This paragraph is all screwed up. It's not right at all.

   Manager B: Hey, this is much better than your last report. Let's figure out what you can do to carry this improvement along even further.

4. *Employee:* Hey, I know how to use that spread sheet. We learned it in the training course I just took.

   Manager A: Well, I'm glad to see that all the time you spent away from the job wasn't a total waste of time. Something did sink in.

   Manager B: Good. I can see you're really relating what you learned in class to what you need on the job.

"That's the easiest exam I ever took," Tim said, laughing. "There's no doubt about *those* answers."

"Okay, wise guy, we'll give you a harder one. Here are three situations. You tell us what the standard (nonreinforcing) response would be, and then give a good reinforcement as the alternative."

REINFORCEMENT EXERCISES

1. You go away on vacation and come back to find that your secretary has cleaned up your desk top and "organized" your in-box. In the process, an important message has been lost.
2. You overhear an employee explaining a procedure to a co-worker.
3. One of your employees refuses to use a method that's been given to her. "It'll never work for me," she says adamantly.

Now list some situations that could arise with your own employees at your own work place. What would the careless response be? How could you meet the situation with a positive reinforcement instead?

TRACKING THE SUCCESS OF REINFORCEMENT

"One more good thing about what you call intangible reinforcement," Tim said, "is that nobody can take it away. I've put my neck in a noose more than once, getting an employee some special pay or benefit and then seen a directive from upstairs take it away again. Boy, that puts you in real trouble with your people!" He thought for a minute. "I'm assuming, you understand, that intangible reinforcement really works. How can you tell, anyway? How do you know that these reinforcers you hand out have any effect?"

"That's just how you can tell, Tim. By the effect they have. And you can almost always see it. If you go back to the feedback graph we made, you can find the places that show you graphically how the reinforcement you give is working—or *if* it's working. Let's look at the graph."

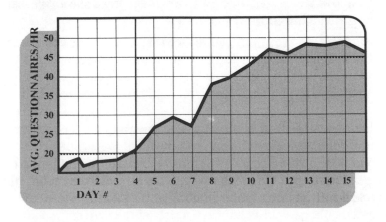

"See what happens in weeks five to ten? You've apparently been reinforcing this employee for her work; she's shown a dramatic improvement over the five weeks. Then, in the next five, it levels out, but it's at or above your goal, so you have no complaint. You could try giving reinforcement less often then.

"On the other hand, suppose the chart looked like this:

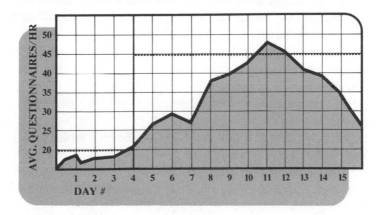

"Something has gone wrong here. Maybe the reinforcers you were giving her lost their effectiveness along about the twelfth week. Or maybe some other variable is preventing her from performing as well as you'd like her to.

"You should also be aware of a third possibility, Tim—that the reinforcement isn't working. Because it doesn't always."

"How come? I'd think that if it can have such spectacular effects in some cases, it would work to a certain extent in every case."

WHY REINFORCEMENT SOMETIMES FAILS

There are several reasons why reinforcement doesn't always work. We listed some of them for Tim.

1. A lot of the time it's something the manager is doing. Take this for example: A manager comes up to an employee and says, 'Hey, that was a great job you did on the research project. The only problem was, it took a helluva long time to wrap up. Don't you think next time you could write your report a little faster?'

   We call that the drop-the-other-shoe syndrome. These employees have been around their manager long enough to know that every ounce of praise will be immediately followed by a pound of criticism. As a result, when this manager says something complimentary, the employees grit their teeth and wait for the ax to fall. Don't earn yourself that kind of a reputation. Praise should be unconditional. When you give reinforcement, you do not want your people to hold their breath and wait for you to say, "And now the bad news. . ."

2. A sudden and suspicious change in a manager's behavior can also account for the failure of reinforcement. Here's a manager who's always been hard to get along with. He's sarcastic, he's overly critical, he makes his employees feel like idiots, he tells them they're in danger of losing their jobs, and he is just generally unpleasant. Then he goes to a management seminar looking like Mr. Hyde and returns acting like Dr. Jekyll. Suddenly he's Mr. Nice Guy. "That's a swell job you did there, Ken," and "You've got terrific sales ability, Louise," and "That's great advice, Bob. Thanks for letting me have it."

   What's going on here? His people ask one another, are we supposed to take this change of heart seriously? Ha! We know him. This transformation won't last a week.

   It's going to take a lot of really sincere positive management on the part of this manager before his employees begin to take his compliments seriously.

3. Reinforcement won't work on behavior that doesn't occur very often. You may commend someone for doing a good job, but if the employee doesn't do that same thing for another eight months, the reinforcement isn't going to carry over. Reinforce tasks that your employees perform regularly.

4. You may have chosen an inappropriate reinforcer. It doesn't give Frank much satisfaction to be invited to a departmental meeting if he doesn't think it's an honor or privilege. If he finds the meetings boring and resents the time he has to spend away from his work, it's no reinforcement. In addition, he may see the invitation as an order to go to a meeting where nobody pays much attention to him.

5. Someone or something may be undermining your attempts at reinforcement. For example, perhaps Frank *does* like to go to those departmental meetings, but his fellow employees make him feel that he is currying favor with the bosses. In this situation, the co-workers' criticism cancels out the manager's reward.

"On the other hand," we told Tim, "it might just be that the reinforcement is working, but you just can't see the results right away. That happens. So don't give up too soon. Your reinforcement may pay off in the long run even if it seems to have failed in the short run."

Talking It Out

Sherman, the manager of a large convention center in the Northeast, is unhappy with the erratic performance of his administrative assistant. Tired of criticizing her and getting no improvement, he decides to talk the problem out with Paul, the manager of the convention center's hotel facility.

SHERMAN   Paul, do you remember last year when you were having so much trouble with that new room clerk of yours, the one who fouled up so many reservations?

PAUL   That was Philip. Of course I remember. It took a while but we got everything straightened out. He's doing all right now.

SHERMAN   I know; that's why I want to talk with you. I'm having a terrible time with my assistant, Amy Travis. She seems to be making a lot of the same mistakes Philip made when he first started working here.

PAUL   What's she doing right?

SHERMAN   She's messing up the floor plans about half of the time.

PAUL   No, Sherman, I didn't ask what she was doing wrong. I want to know what she's doing right.

SHERMAN   Why do you want to know that? It's what she does wrong that bothers me. During the software conference two weeks ago, she had the concessionaires at one another's throats because she had sent out conflicting directions on the locations of various booths. It took a lot of persuasion on my part to get everybody calmed down and settled.

PAUL   Yes, I heard about that. And yet the mining engineers' conference last week seemed to go off without a hitch. Was she in charge of that floor?

SHERMAN   Yes, and she did a terrific job. The plan was flawless, and she kept moving around, talking to people, seeing to it that they had everything they needed. They were delighted with her, and I was very pleased with her performance on that job.

PAUL   So, in other words, Amy does do something right, doesn't she? Did you tell her how pleased you were?

SHERMAN   Yes, and I'm afraid that was a mistake. You see, I chewed her out good for blundering on the software conference, and she pulled herself together a bit for the mining people. Then I praised her, unwisely, I guess—because she turned right around and bungled up the seminar schedule for tomorrow's medical association meeting. You see? I can't count on her to do steady good work. How did you get Philip to pull himself together?

PAUL   By praising him when he did something right. In the beginning I had to look hard to find something to praise, because he was all thumbs until he got a feel for the job. But every time he handled a guest's complaint tactfully or straightened out a reservation problem, I laid on the praise. Gradually, he began to pull himself together, as you said. He seemed to be trying hard to earn my praise, and being extra careful not to make mistakes that would cause me to withhold my compliments. Maybe you should take that approach with Amy.

SHERMAN   But I did praise her for the miners' meeting, and she turned right around and blew the next conference. So my reward backfired, didn't it?

PAUL   Not necessarily. Amy is new here, and she has a complex set of responsibilities. You've been on the job for seven years, so you understand all of the nuances that are still unfamiliar to her. Try to look at things from her point of view. She's bound to make a number of mistakes at first. Chances are, she feels terrible about messing up the schedule for the medical convention. Did you criticize her for that mistake?

SHERMAN   You bet I did. I was so furious I nearly fired her on the spot.

PAUL   And how did she respond to your criticism?

SHERMAN   She got very upset, apologized all over the place, tried to explain what had happened, seemed to be very nervous and jittery.

PAUL   You don't suppose she's feeling so pressured to perform that she's self-destructing, do you? Maybe she's so terrified of being yelled at that she's not thinking straight.

SHERMAN   Come on, Paul. You make me sound like an ogre. I don't pick on her all the time—only when she does something wrong.

PAUL   Which is quite often, right?

SHERMAN   Right. I guess I spend way too much time correcting her.

PAUL   Why not give her a chance to earn your praise enough times to build up her confidence in her own ability to do the job? You said yourself that she did a great job at the miners' meeting. Wait and see what happens tomorrow. If she gets the booths ready in time for the first visitors, praise her for that. Don't mention the scheduling problem. That's over and done with; forget it. Find something you like about her work, and let her know about it. Tell her when she has a good day, not when she's met a failure; she probably feels bad enough about that already.

SHERMAN   I don't know, Paul. Praise works on some people, but it doesn't seem to work on Amy. Look what happened the last time I praised her.

PAUL   You mean the _only_ time you praised her. You have to keep it up, Sherman. If you tell her how pleased you are when she does well, she'll feel good. She'll try to earn your praise again and again. If you keep telling her how bad she is over and over, she'll just get discouraged. She'll say, "I can't please him no matter how hard I try, so why bother to try?"

SHERMAN   Then I really will fire her.

PAUL   But wouldn't you rather keep her? From what you've said, I get the feeling that Amy has all kinds of potential. She can organize a concession floor, as she did for the miners. And she apparently did a good job on scheduling for both the miners and the software group. And you say she seems to get along well with people. Why let her go? You might not be able to find another assistant with those good qualities.

SHERMAN   She does have a lot to offer. She's so pleasant to the guests, and she's cool and poised. And you're right—she pulls most of the planning jobs off without a hitch. Maybe she just needs some time and some help getting the procedures down pat. She can be very efficient when she wants to.

PAUL   Then it's up to you to see that she _wants_ to be efficient all the time. And the way to do that is to tell her what a help she is to you when she does her best. Anyone would tend to be clumsy in the early days on a job. When Amy does something clumsy, maybe you could remind her of something wonderful she did the day before. Just keep telling her when she does well.

SHERMAN   That's how you helped Philip when he first started working at the desk, right? You kept looking for the things he did right?

PAUL Exactly, as I said. After a while, he began to do more and more things right until eventually he was doing almost everything right, and getting more and more praise all the time.

SHERMAN So he did have the ability, even though he appeared not to at first. You just made him want to work at the peak of his ability all the time.

PAUL That's it. And the technique worked—not immediately, as you know, but after a fair trial period.

SHERMAN You know, I'm glad I talked to you about this, Paul. You've helped me see that I've been too impatient. I'll try your technique. I think Amy has the ability to be a fine assistant; in fact, I'm sure of it.

PAUL Then it's your job to get her to use her ability all the time instead of just once in a while.

SHERMAN I appreciate the management lesson, Paul. I'm going to praise, praise, praise. I'll let you know later on whether the technique works for me or not.

PAUL It will work, Sherman. That's a promise. It works with room clerks, housecleaning personnel, security people, and office staff. It'll work like a charm with Amy, too. You'll see.

SHERMAN I believe it. Thanks again.

CHAPTER 9

PICK YOURSELF A PIC: THE BALANCE-OF-CONSEQUENCES ANALYSIS

"I knew it was going to happen, because we've been practicing for it all year."

   —First grader, commenting on a fire at her school

"What you win in New York you lose in Chicago."

   —Ernest Hemingway

"**B**EHAVIOR MODIFICATION?" TIM SAID. "I DON'T know—are you sure it's not some kind of brainwashing?"

We laughed. "Hardly. It's a quite beneficial process; a helpful way to reward people. It also makes them give their best to a job and get the most satisfaction out of doing it."

"How does it work?"

"It's really very simple. We've talked about ROI, and you know that it's an effective tool for managing through goal-setting. The Two-to-Four-Minute Feedback session is a means of answering the employee's often unspoken but very urgent question, 'How am I doing?' Now, to help you manage through rewards, there's another extremely effective technique—behavior modifications. Faced with an employee who's doing something wrong, a manager can use this technique to analyze the consequences of the worker's current undesired behavior as well as the consequences of the desired behavior the manager wishes to substitute. Once the analysis is complete, the manager will usually be able to see how behavior modification can change the minuses to pluses."

THE BALANCE-OF-CONSEQUENCES ANALYSIS

As an example, let's take the case of Ed Carlton, a certified public accountant who works for a large automotive parts company. His job is to travel around to the firm's numerous franchised dealerships and conduct audits of each dealer's books.

Carlton enjoys the traveling. He's very gregarious and has made friends with all the dealers and their employees. He gets great pleasure out of his visits with them. But his very sociability has created a problem: Ed spends a great deal of time chatting with the dealership employees and frequently involves himself in problems of theirs that have nothing to do with his job. Consequently, it takes him 50 percent longer to complete an audit than it does his fellow accountants in the same kind of work.

Carlton's manager, Lisa McCormick, definitely doesn't want to lose Ed. He's an excellent and skilled accountant, and his friendliness, helpfulness, and popularity make him an asset to the company; the good feeling the dealers have for him spills over to the organization he represents. But his low productivity is decidedly uneconomic.

Lisa recently finished a company course in behavior modification, and she decided to analyze Ed's problem using a technique she has just learned. She now knows that a manager analyzing the consequences of an employee's behavior should try to put herself in the employee's place. That way, the manager will see the consequences as the employee sees them. So, putting herself in Carlton's place, Lisa listed all the consequences she could think of. Her list included all the rewards and punishments that could result from Ed's current, undesired behavior. Here is her list:

- Ed enjoys socializing with the dealers and their employees.
- Ed gains satisfaction from the knowledge that the dealership people like him very much.
- Ed earns praise and appreciation from dealers for solving their problems.
- The dealers report back to the home office that Ed is friendly and willing to help them; as a result, he gets praised by his supervisors.

Against this list of rewards, Lisa itemized the punishing consequences of Ed's current behavior:

- The company's comptroller constantly complains that Ed takes too long to complete his audits.
- Ed often has to work overtime because he spends so much of the workday socializing.
- His chances for promotion are diminished because he is so slow in completing his audits.

Now Lisa lists the desirable consequences that will ensue if Ed Carlton changes his behavior. If he spends less time socializing with the dealers and concentrates more on the audits he is being paid to make, Lisa figures he'll gain the following rewards:

- He'll be able to say good-bye to home office criticism for slow work.
- His chances for promotion will increase.
- He won't have to work so much overtime.

But here's how he might lose by the change:

- He'll miss out on the good times he now has chatting with dealership employees.
- He'll have more actual work to do—more traveling and more audits.
- He'll lose some of the admiration and appreciation he is currently getting.

Lisa made a chart, as she had been taught, listing those consequences in relevant sections of it:

BEHAVIOR

UNDESIRED (Current)	DESIRED

REINFORCING CONSEQUENCES

#1 Pleasant socializing during visits

#2 Admiration and appreciation from dealership people

#3 Praise and appreciation for solving dealers' problems

#4 Good reports to the home office

#1 End of criticism from home office

#2 Increased chances for promotion

#3 Less overtime

PUNISHING CONSEQUENCES

#1 Constant complaints from comptroller

#2 Lots of overtime

#3 Decreased chances for promotion

#1 Less pleasant socializing

#2 More traveling, more audits, more work

#3 Loss of some admiration and appreciation

In her behavior modification course, Lisa had learned that all consequences fall into one of three either/or categories. Every consequence is either:

- Personal or Organizational
- Immediate or Delayed
- Certain or Uncertain (Gamble)

Lisa took a hard look at these different kinds of consequences and determined which category each one on her chart fell into. A consequence that benefits the individual rather than the company is personal rather than organizational. Lisa saw immediately that all of Ed's actions produced personal consequences. Each one of his actions, in other words, either pleased him personally or hurt him. On her chart, therefore, she labeled each consequence *P* for Personal.

In studying the timeliness of the consequences of Ed's behavior, Lisa found more variety. Some of Ed's actions produced immediate gratification. He was, for instance, immediately rewarded with smiles and compliments when he talked and laughed with the dealership employees; Lisa labeled that consequence *I*, for Immediate. Other consequences, however, did not occur until days, weeks, or even months after the action that produced them—the comptroller's complaints, for example. She labeled that consequence *D* for Delayed. Lisa studied the list carefully, labeling some consequences *I* and others *D*.

That done, she examined the consequences to determine how much risk each one involved: How much of a gamble was Ed taking by indulging in each behavior? By chatting and laughing with dealership employees and involving himself in their problems, Ed *knew* he would earn their admiration, so the consequence of that action was certain; Lisa labeled it *C*, because no risk was involved. At the same time, however, while he chatted and laughed, he took a risk of decreasing his chances for promotion. Maybe he could get away with this behavior; maybe he couldn't. Lisa labeled that consequence *G*, for Gamble.

When Lisa had analyzed all of the consequences on the basis of these three either/or categories, her chart looked like this:

BEHAVIOR

UNDESIRED (Current)		DESIRED	
REINFORCING CONSEQUENCES			
#1 Pleasant socializing during visits	PIC	#1 End of criticism from home office	PDC
#2 Admiration and appreciation from dealership people		#2 Increased chances for promotion	PDG
#3 Praise and appreciation for solving dealers' problems	PIC	#3 Less overtime	PDC
#4 Good reports to the home office.	PDG		
PUNISHING CONSEQUENCES			
#1 Constant complaints from comptroller	PIC	#1 Less pleasant socializing	PIG
#2 Lots of overtime	PDG	#2 More traveling, more audits, more work	PDC
#3 Decreased chances for promotion	PDG	#3 Loss of some admiration and appreciation	PDG

Looking at the undesired (current) side of the chart, we see right away Ed is being rewarded for behavior that his manager and the company regard as a problem. If he changes, he will suffer all the punishing consequences of what Lisa wants him to do. In other words, by changing, Ed will get the opposite of what he likes and wants.

Clearly, the manager has to make some changes here. She has to ask herself which of the three either/or factors Ed values most: personal or organizational; immediate or delayed; certain or a gamble. Which kinds of rewards have the greatest effect on his behavior?

Personal consequences are bound to be the most powerful. People care more about what happens to themselves than about what happens to their organization or to the people they work with. Immediate rewards are more effective than delayed consequences. And most people prefer a certainty to a gamble.

Make up a similar chart dealing with one of your own "problem" employees. List as many consequences of both the problem behavior and the desired behavior—both reinforcers and punishers. Then analyze them, marking them P or O; I or D; C or G.

"How," we asked Tim, "would you go about changing this employee's performance in view of the consequences we've seen and analyzed?"

"Let's see. Maybe I'd talk to the comptroller about finding a way to reinforce the guy instead of putting him down by nagging and criticizing him. Maybe if he gets more praise from the home office, he won't need so much of it from the dealers."

"Right. That's certainly one thing you can do, and it's a good one."

Change the balance of consequences so that the employee is rewarded for desired behavior and punished for undesired behavior—not the other way around.

As you can see a manager could change the balance of consequences of the desired behavior by (1) adding positive consequences, or (2) removing negative consequences. You can change the balance of consequences of the undesired behavior by (1) removing positive consequences, or, as a last resort, (2) adding punishing consequences. You could also try changing the dimensions of some of the consequences: Make a delayed consequence more immediate, for example, or see to it that a gamble is more certain to take place.

Here's an interesting example of balance-of-consequence adjustment in a real situation. We call it the Case of the Missing Job Tickets—although there's hardly a mystery about where they are.

A tool and engineering company was having difficulty getting the toolmakers to turn in their job tickets. The firm does initial rough estimates, estimates the job more thoroughly once it is in the shop, and then draws up job tickets for each employee to fill out as he carries out his assignments. In this way, management can keep track of the actual cost of the labor. If, for example, a piece is worked on for three hours on the bench, two on the grinder, an hour and a half on the lathe, and six hours on the drill, the job tickets should reflect that. Management uses the job tickets to determine the accuracy of estimate and to decide how much to bid for new jobs.

The toolmakers, however, were not filling out their job tickets. Many of the employees regarded the job tickets as a nuisance, and neglected filling them out. Their immediate supervisors consequently had to spend a lot of time each day going from one toolmaker to another urging that he fill out the ticket.

To avoid wasting time in this way, the managers would get on the loud-speaker every morning and read off the names of those toolmakers who did not fill out their job tickets the day before. Each one was asked to report to the office to fill out the previous day's job tickets.

Here are the consequences the men faced for *not* filling out the job tickets on time:

- Filling out the job tickets on time meant staying in the shop a few minutes past quitting time. By failing to complete the tickets, the men were able to leave work on time and thus avoid getting caught in a small traffic tie-up as the plant let out.
- Toolmakers sometimes got chewed out by their managers for not completing the job tickets.
- Toolmakers who did not fill out their job tickets were given ten minutes to do so the next morning.
- The names of the negligent toolmakers were announced over the loudspeaker.
- The tardy filler-outers got a lot of good-natured razzing—*and* a lot of attention—from their co-workers when their names were read over the speaker system.
- If the job tickets were incomplete or incorrect, the company could lose work due to misbidding.
- Incomplete job tickets made it difficult to schedule work because the company did not have accurate or complete information.

We asked Tim to divide this list of consequences into punishments and reinforcers for desired and undesired behavior. He came up with these conclusions.

The undesired behavior is reinforced by three of the conseqeucnes: (1) the workers get ten minutes in the morning to fill in the job tickets and consequently that much time away from their work; (2) they can leave work on time, thus avoiding the traffic jam; and (3) they earn the attention of their co-workers, who razz them in a good-natured way when their names are read over the speaker system.

The undesired behavior is punished by four of the consequences: (1) the workers sometimes get chewed out by management; (2) they know they're causing a potential loss of work to that company; (3) they risk losing income by not helping the company determine the costs of each job; and (4) their own work becomes more difficult to schedule.

What about the desired behavior—the toolmakers completing their job tickets accurately at the end of work each day? There are *no* reinforcing consequences for this: only punishing ones. The employees who comply with this rule have to stay past quitting time to fill in their job tickets. Consequently they face a traffic jam on leaving. And they don't get ten minutes off the next morning.

Now let's rate these consequences as either personal or organizational, immediate or delayed, certain or a gamble. We find that all of the consequences are personal except the potential loss of work, the possibility of getting the work but losing money on it, and the difficulty in scheduling—all of which are organizational, delayed, and uncertain (gambles). The finished balance-of-consequences analysis looks like this:

BEHAVIOR

UNDESIRED (Current)		DESIRED	
REINFORCING CONSEQUENCES			
#1 Ten minutes away from from the job each morning	PDC	NONE!	
#2 Names announced on loudspeakers	PIC		
#3 Clapping and cheering of co-workers	PIC		
PUNISHING CONSEQUENCES			
#1 Getting chewed out by management	PIG/PDG	#1 Having to stay past quitting time	PIC
#2 Potential loss of work by company	ODG	#2 Getting caught in traffic jam	PIC
#3 Scheduling problems	ODC/OIC		

Notice that a consequence can have more than one set of dimensions.

Tim looked at the chart. "That's a pretty uneven balance," he said.

"Yes, it is. You can sympathize with the toolmakers for not wanting to bother with the job tickets. What's in it for them? There are no rewards, and only one of the punishing consequences affects them directly, personally, and immediately—getting bawled out by their managers—but that doesn't leave many skilled workers trembling in their boots in this day and age. Could you add some positive consequences for the behavior you're trying to get?"

"Well," Tim said after some thought, "I'd certainly tell them how great they are for filling out their job tickets accurately and on time on the occasions when they do it, even if it's only every now and then."

"Right, Tim. Now, how could you remove the punishing consequences of the behavior you're looking for?"

"I'd give my employees the last ten minutes of the working day to fill out the forms," Tim said. "What do I have to lose? They're already taking ten minutes out of their working day to do it, only at a less convenient time. If they take the same ten minutes in the morning, they can avoid the traffic jam and get out on time. I'd gain a lot, too, because I wouldn't have to spend time nagging them to get their tickets done."

"You know, Tim," we told him, "these talks we're having are really paying off. You're getting to think more and more like a positive manager."

"Aw, go on," he said. "You're just reinforcing me."

"Okay, student, next test coming up. How could you remove the reinforcing consequences of the toolmakers' undesirable behavior?"

"I wouldn't give my people time to fill in their job tickets in the morning," Tim said. "They'd have to do it on their own time; I wouldn't let them punch in until it was done.

"Also, I wouldn't give them the thrill of hearing their names on the loudspeakers, and that would mean they wouldn't get all that good-natured razzing and cheering from the other workers."

"Suppose you took all of those actions, Tim, and they didn't work. Then what would you do?"

"Then I'd have to take drastic steps—punishment, but only as a last resort. I'd dock the people who wouldn't cooperate, or even fire them if I had to."

"Okay. It's head of the class for you. Incidentally, another thing you could do is change the dimensions of the consequences by making it clear to your employees how the consequences to the organization have an effect on them. If the company loses money or loses work, eventually the toolmakers are going to be laid off. If the firm has scheduling problems, everybody's work suffers, and again, the company is going to suffer economically, which will hurt the employees."

"You know that old saying," Tim said thoughtfully, "you can catch more flies with honey than you can with vinegar. That's really true in managing, isn't it? I know some of us managers don't pay much attention to our people as long as they're performing well. The only time we notice their work is when it's wrong, and then we light into the person we think is responsible. Which usually just makes things worse."

"Managers have another tendency worth mentioning here, Tim. They often manage by antecedents, when they should be doing it by *consequences*. In his work on behavior modification, B.F. Skinner concluded that 'behavior is a function of its consequences.' In other words, the consequences shape the behavior."

"What are antecedents?"

"They're part of the ABCs of behavior. Antecedent is the *A*, something that precedes the behavior and gets it started. The *B* is the behavior itself, and the *C* is the consequences. A lot of managers will try to get the behavior they want by giving orders, holding policy meetings, and setting up training courses. Those things are good, sure, but they're all antecedents; they *precede* behavior. Much more effective are the actions that maintain behavior once it's been started, and keep it going—the consequences.

"Remember Edward J. Feeney of Emery Air Freight, the executive who found a way to get his warehouse employee to make better use of large containers? Well, ten years ago, Feeney pioneered the use of positive reinforcement at his company—and cut costs by $2 million a year. Now a number of other companies are using behavior modification. According to *Business Week* magazine, those organizations have had sizable cost savings, huge gains in productivity and at least a 200 percent return on investment. Those are impressive results."

"I'm impressed," said Tim.

As a manager, how many of these actions do you take to increase the performance of your employees?

1. Set goals
2. Run a contest
3. Post figures for performance by individuals or teams
4. Give praise for good performance
5. Threaten
6. Provide training
7. Send complimentary memos to employees

Which of these actions are antecedents, and which are consequences? Mark each item on the above list.*

---

*1, 2, and 6 are antecedents; 5 could be either one; 3, 4, and 7 are consequences.

Make a list of any additional actions you take to improve the performance of your employees, labeling them *A* for antecedents or *C* for consequences.

"Basically, then, positive managing hinges on rewarding people for good performance, right?" Tim asked.

"That's only one of four main techniques of behavior modification that you have available to you. We've talked a good bit about rewards, both material and psychological. Then there is their opposite—punishment.

"Punishment. Now, how, short of docking someone's pay or firing the person—both of which are pretty drastic—would you go about punishing one of your employees? It sounds as if you're going to make the offender sit in the corner, or take away the car keys for a week."

"It's not that—and it's not forty lashes with a cat-o'-nine-tails, either. There are other ways to punish, as I'm sure you know."

"Me?"

"Haven't you ever kept information from someone, or ignored a job that someone had done very well because you were annoyed with that person for some reason? Haven't you ever criticized an employee in front of others—even ridiculed her or him? You can deliberately delay a person's vacation or be extra picky over an expense account or duck out of talking to the employee about an expected raise. Sometimes a thoughtless manager even punishes an employee for doing something especially good."

"That sounds crazy."

"Think about it. What about a very effective and fast employee who finishes her work ahead of everyone else—and is then given everyone else's work to finish? She is penalized for being fast and effective; she's given more work to do than the other employees. And what about that ubiquitous office rule—'first one in makes the coffee'?"

"You know, you're right. I'm guilty of things like that occasionally, too."

"You're less guilty than a lot of people, Tim. You're a smart manager, and you know without anyone having to tell you that, on the whole, punishment is counterproductive. It makes people resentful. They're either ready to fight you at every turn or else they just turn themselves off and do as little as possible."

Some employees regard punishment as a kind of reward, as we mentioned earlier. Employees hungry for attention perversely enjoy being singled out for punishment. And, of course, punishment is nonproductive in the end, because if you remove the punishment, the undesired behavior will be repeated. You'll have to keep an eagle eye on employees you punish.

"There's something else," Tim said. "I don't want my people to see me as some kind of ogre. When I come around, I don't want them to be waiting for me to criticize them or put them down."

"Right. You also have to remember that the person being punished might whip up sympathy among the other employees. If that happens, you could have an epidemic of bad feeling on your hands."

"But what if I catch some guy messing around with the machinery and making things dangerous for some of the others on the floor?"

"Then, of course, you've *got* to punish. When lives are being endangered, or you catch someone stealing money from the company, then you've got to fall back on severe measures like suspension or dismissal. But in most other cases, instead of punishment, it's smart to reinforce positive behavior and reduce the reinforcement the employee is getting for undesired behavior. You know, when baby starts to teethe on Grandpa's gold watch, we take the watch away and give baby a cookie. The cookie serves to neutralize the undesired effects of punishment. And this works just as well with adults. It just takes a bit more imagination to find the grown-up equivalent of the cookie."

"Rewards and punishment. That's two behavior modification techniques. What's the third one?"

"The third technique is *extinction*."

"There you go again. Does that mean the manager is an endangered species?"

We laughed. "Not the *positive* manager! No, we're not talking about extinguishing the manager—just the reward for undesired behavior."

Your employee persists in behavior that you would like to change because they get some kind of reinforcement for it. It has some consequence that makes them want to continue it. If you're using the technique of extinction, you first find out what that reinforcement is and then, if possible, extinguish it—take it away.

However, this is a long process, compared to some of the other techniques. And if at the same time the employee is getting reinforcement from some other source, either outside or inside the work place, your withholding the reinforcement won't succeed in getting rid of the undesired behavior. It might weaken, but it won't disappear.

"So what do we do instead?"

"We use all the techniques we've learned up until now—reinforcement, punishment, and extinction—to get the fourth behavior modification technique. It's called *shaping*."

Shaping is reinforcing step-by-step improvement toward the kind of behavior you are hoping for. It is the ideal way to deal with complex behavior patterns, because the technique breaks them down into steps. You reinforce each step as the employee progresses toward the desired behavior. Shaping gives you an opportunity to control the development of a complex skill until it is fully mastered. If you go about it sensibly, one step at a time, you will soon learn how far you can direct each step so that the employee must stretch to do just a bit more than is comfortable, but is not pushed ahead so quickly that he or she feels tense and frustrated.

Six top executives of a large company had an experience with their electronic data processing manager that illustrates the shaping technique.

These six executives were supposed to get a daily computer printout at 8:45 A.M. It was important that they see the printout at that time, because it had an important bearing on their day's activities.

Actually, the printout rarely got to them before 9:30 A.M. and it was frequently incomplete. Instead of demanding that the EDP manager start delivering the data forty-five minutes earlier, the managers asked him to get the printout to their offices by 9:00 rather than 9:30. He agreed to try.

The printouts didn't start coming in at nine every day immediately, but when they did arrive on time, the executives made a point of complimenting the EDP manager on the improvement and telling him how much of a help it was to everyone to receive the printout earlier. Little by little the printouts began to come in consistently at 9:00—sometimes even a bit earlier.

At that point, the executives had another meeting with the EDP manager. "Since you've been able to get the printout to us by nine very consistently," they said, "it would really be great if you could try to pull it to the original target of 8:45. That extra fifteen minutes could make a lot of difference to us. Do you think you could do it?"

"Yes," the EDP manager answered. "I think so. In trying to get it to you by nine, I learned some ways to get it out faster." With continuing reinforcement, the printouts began arriving regularly at 8:45.

With that much accomplished, the executives used the same shaping approach to solve the problem of incomplete printouts. That worked, too, in a reasonable period of time.

GUIDELINES FOR EFFECTIVE SHAPING

- Reinforce the desired behavior *immediately*.
- Be specific. Make sure the employee knows which behavior you are reinforcing.
- Ignore poor performances.

- At first, reinforce an action that is easily accomplished and that is close to the behavior you want. Later, lessen the distance between what you are getting and the desired behavior. Keep raising your standards as the exercise continues, reinforcing only what is close to what you really want.
- Make the reinforcement as personal as possible.

Shaping takes time, but the results are worthwhile.

Talking It Out

Two sales managers from different companies have met at a sales rally on the Gulf Coast. They're having an after-dinner drink together on the terrace of the hotel, which is crowded with sales people who have come from all over the United States to attend the rally.

JOEL   Yes, I must say that my people are pretty terrific, for the most part.

ALAN   For the most part? You mean you have one or two who give you trouble?

JOEL   I have one who tries my patience to the limit. He's standing over there by the palm tree. See him? The one in the navy blue blazer with the red necktie. That's Bob Thorndike.

ALAN   Oh, he's one of your people? I've been watching him for two days, thinking he must be a hell of a good salesman. He's always surrounded by people. In fact, he seems to be holding court over there right now. Looks to me like a natural for the job. What's his problem?

JOEL   Inconsistency, mostly. When he's on a roll, he's one of my best people. But, unfortunately, he doesn't stay on a roll for very long. Every once in a while I send him to rallies like this one, and he comes home and sells up a storm for a couple of months. Then he slowly sinks into relative inactivity, and I have to send him to another rally to get him back into shape. It's getting mighty expensive to keep him performing at the level I know he's capable of achieving.

ALAN   Hmm, an interesting problem. When he's on one of his rolls, does he generate new business?

JOEL   Yes, he brings in about one out of five of the accounts he goes after, which is a good sales rate. But then, after a while, he seems to run out of steam, and he starts to just coast along again, not bringing in much of anything.

ALAN   You say he gets one account out of five. You see that as a good rate, but maybe he sees it the other way around, Joel. He thinks of it as losing four out of five sales rather than winning four out of five. Maybe that's what makes him run out of steam after a couple of months.

JOEL   I never thought of that possibility, but you could be right. I see the glass as half full, but maybe he sees it as half empty. That's a good point.

ALAN   During those slumps of his, when he doesn't bring in any new business, how do you handle him?

JOEL   I try not to be too rough on him, but I do sit him down in my office and talk to him privately—sometimes at considerable length.

ALAN   Does he resent that?

JOEL   Not at all. In fact, he seems to appreciate my spending so much time with him.

ALAN   Do you ever sit him down in your office when he's on a roll?

JOEL   Uh-oh, I see what you're getting at, Alan. No, I never have a long talk with him when he's doing well, only when he's in a slump. I never realized that before, but now I know exactly what you mean. Bob Thorndike absolutely thrives on attention. You can see that by the way he's behaving at this rally. And the only way he can get attention from me is to fail. Boy, have I made a blunder! I've been rewarding him with attention whenever he does poor work.

ALAN   Don't be so hard on yourself, Joel. You're so close to the problem that you can't see it clearly. If you could step back from the situation, you'd see that you're doing something else to reinforce his poor performance. Do you know what that is?

JOEL   You mean I'm rewarding poor performance in some other way—besides paying extra attention to him?

ALAN   You sure are. When he gets so deep into a slump that a fatherly chat won't pull him out of it, then what do you do, Joel?

JOEL   I send him on a tropical vacation—to a sales rally like this one! You're right again, Alan; I'm rewarding Bob handsomely for doing poor work. First I give him my full attention. Then I pack him off to some sandy beach. No wonder he goes into a slump every four months. I'd probably do the same thing if my boss repaid me so well for it. I might just as well have walked up to him and said, "Bob, you've done a terrific job lately, so I'm going to reward you by sending you to Florida." Boy, do I feel stupid.

ALAN   Don't blame yourself. As I said before, it's hard to see things clearly when you're so close to the problem. You have to step back and look at the consequences of your actions as well as Bob's. Then you take some time to study the way those consequences balance one another. Now that you know how your actions have affected Bob's performance, you can decide what you have to do differently from now on. You'll also see how Bob's actions result in certain predictable consequences, tempting him to repeat those actions over and over.

JOEL   Right. From now on I'll make these sales rallies a reward for good work, not poor performance. I'll set a specific sales goal for Bob to reach, and I'll reward him with a trip if he accomplishes that goal on time.

ALAN   You could also just ignore him when his sales begin to slip. And call him into your office only when he's doing really well.

JOEL   And I can help him to see that he's selling one client out of five, not losing four out of five.

ALAN   I think you'll solve Bob's problems in short order. And remember, you can use the same basic techniques for other problems you may run up against with your employees. Give the trouble a good hard look and determine the consequences of every action—good and bad, positive and negative. Then decide how those consequences balance out. That'll help you to see things you've been overlooking.

JOEL   I'll certainly do that, and thanks a lot. I'm glad I ran into you. And I think in the long run Bob will be glad, too.

CHAPTER 10

ARE YOU WITH ME? MANAGING THROUGH THE INFLUENCE OF SUPPORT

"There are just three things I'd ever say: If anything goes bad, *I* did it; if anything goes semi-good, then *we* did it; if anything goes real good, then *you* did it. That's all it takes to get people to win football games for you."

—*Bear Bryant*

WHAT HAPPENS WHEN AN EMPLOYEE NEEDS HELP? A positive manager will say that the employee should seek help from the manager. And if the top managers support their middle managers, they will have given some thought to problems they can expect to arise.

At Disneyland, employees are urged to treat customers as though they were guests in the employees' homes. This is effective, but even the best-intentioned guide or service person finds it difficult to be "good" all the time. So Disneyland developed the concept of "off-stage" and "on-stage behavior. The standards for on-stage behavior are obvious. To counterbalance the stress of maintaining those standards, the company created an off-stage area where employees are given free rein to rid themselves of tension in an acceptable way—by hitting a rubber dummy or an old tire with a baseball bat, by screaming and yelling, or by some form of intense physical exertion.

The Japanese version of a coffee break in many companies in that country is a time that is structured for relaxation and for activities that release tension. Often the breaks involve exercise sessions or some form of meditation. Such planning demonstrates the organization's understanding and support of the individual worker.

Does the manager always come through with support and understanding? No, for one or more reasons. Let's look at three situations where, for different reasons, employees did *not* get help and support from their managers.

THE MANAGER WHO WITHHOLDS SUPPORT

Walter Gresham, a claims adjuster for an automobile insurance company, was so good at his job that he was penalized by getting extra work to do.

Walter was by far the most effective adjuster in his department—highly competent, skilled, excellent with people. Recognizing his ability, his supervisor always saved the toughest problems for Walter. Then, in addition, he would load Gresham with cases that would ordinarily have gone to another employee.

Although Walter was flattered at first to be singled out for his excellent work, that feeling soon gave way to annoyance, and then to anger and stress. Case piled on case; his hours became longer and longer. He also had less time to spend cultivating personal relations with clients, although he was very good at that kind of work and his talent worked to the company's advantage. The quality of his work was deteriorating, and he knew it.

Gresham also knew where help should come from. He went to his manager, explained the situation, and asked that fewer cases be assigned to him so that he could do a better job on the ones he had. The manager said, "We'll see what we can do about it."

What he did was exactly nothing.

Walter kept on trying to cope. Eventually he decided to do a good job on as many cases as possible and just let the rest pile up. But the backlog made him uncomfortable; as a responsible person he was under constant pressure from his own conscience, and he felt terrible about the neglected work. Now, to add insult to injury, the manager started to get on Gresham's back about the backlog. He kept urging Walter to work faster. They argued; there was some name-calling. In the manager's view, Walter had become a problem employee.

When the situation became intolerable, Gresham handed in his resignation. He got another job at a substantial increase in salary, and he is doing extremely well at it—as he could have for his first employer if the manager had provided the support this employee was wise enough to ask for but not lucky enough to get.

THE EMPLOYEE WHO WON'T ASK FOR SUPPORT

Jean-Marie Durand is an electrical engineer who for the last two years has worked as a sales representative for a semiconductor company.

Recently, changes in technology have come so fast that Jean-Marie finds it hard to keep up with them. As a result, she sometimes loses a sale because a competitor's product is at a more advanced state of the art—one she hadn't known about. She's even finding it hard to keep up with her own product line.

Obviously Jean-Marie needs help. Why doesn't she get it? Because she's afraid that if she goes to her manager and tells him what the trouble is, he'll decide that she isn't competent enough to do her job. So she says nothing and struggles along. The truth is that with a little help she'd do a better job for her company as well as for herself.

THE MANAGER WHO IS UNAWARE
OF THE CAUSE OF A PROBLEM

There's bad feeling in the word processing department of a large grocery chain. One of the operators, Denise Coleman, has twice in the past two weeks accidentally erased a large chunk of copy from backup disks in the standard contract file. This fouls things for everyone else in the department. For example, Lucy Alcott, the manager, gets saddled with a load of extra work and problems because of Denise's goofs. Lucy is furious, and the whole department suffers.

What neither woman realizes is that Denise was not trained on the present word processing system. She knew the old one, but she was on vacation when the rest of the staff learned to use the one that was recently installed. When Denise came back, Lucy had one of the other operators break her in on the new equipment. Although the other operator had learned the system well enough to use it, she wasn't much of a teacher. In explaining it to Denise, she left out some important steps and details—with disastrous results. This situation could easily have been remedied by giving Denise a thorough retraining in the new system, but the manager didn't know how inadequate Denise's training had been—and neither did Denise herself. As a result, hostility developed between manager and employee, Denise did poor work, and trouble arose for all concerned.

"There's a lesson in this for you, Tim," we said. "A lot of the time employees won't come to the manager with a problem. They may be afraid of looking incompetent, like Jean-Marie; they may not realize the manager can—or will—help them; or, like Denise, they may not be aware of the nature of the problem and how it could be solved—or even that a problem exists."

"That's a possibility, too. In any case, the responsibility rests with the manager."

"I'm aware that someone just starting out needs plenty of support from the manager," Tim said.

"But people don't remain beginners forever, Tim. Doing a good job is a continuing process. An employee can need help any time. You've got to be alert to I-need-help signals from *all* of your employees—novices and veterans alike. The positive manager is always aware that people have unconscious ways of calling for help. Denise Coleman's two word processing blunders, for instance, were an unconscious cry for help that she didn't even realize she needed. The positive manager would have taken one look at the second blunder and said, 'Uh-oh, Denise needs my help. She's never goofed twice in a row before.'

"Jean-Marie's supervisor—assuming she's lucky enough to work for a positive manager—should hear a cry for help when her sales record falls or when a blank look passes across Jean-Marie's face at the mention of a recent technological development.

"In addition to being alert for unconscious cries for help, the positive manager will always let his or her people know that help is only as far away as the manager's office."

"I guess one thing I should do is make more of a point of telling my people to feel free to come to me with any problems."

What do you do to encourage your employees to bring their problems to you? How do you react when they ask for your help?

A common feeling among employees seems to be apprehension about telling the manager they have a problem. In fact, withholding troublesome information from the boss is an almost universal workplace norm. A positive manager will work to change that norm. Your goal is to convince all of your employees to come to you when they have a problem.

We heard years ago about an eighth grade teacher who had a big sign over her blackboard: It Is Safe to Make a Mistake in This Room. That's the positive workplace norm—exactly the kind you should aim for. Make your employees feel that it's always okay to ask you for help, that it's normal, welcome, even expected.

Here are three things for a manager to keep in mind. They'll help to create an atmosphere that encourages requests for help:

- Remember that your people need your support *all the time*, not just during their first few weeks on the job, and not just during crises.
- Learn to recognize your employees' cries for help—even if the workers aren't aware that they need assistance.
- Continually encourage your people to ask for help when they need it.

"When you get right down to it," Tim Stone said, "just how many kinds of performance problems can be solved by the manager's support?"

BARRIERS TO GOOD PERFORMANCE

We assured Tim that there were a good many such problems. Studies have shown that six barriers to good performance can be overcome with help from the manager. Here are the problems:

1. Employees don't know what is expected of them.
2. They don't know how to do something (frequently because of technological change).
3. They don't *want* to do something.

4. They don't have the proper tools or procedures for the job.

5. They don't know that they aren't performing well.

6. They either don't have the ability to do the job or are overqualified for it.

It is important for you as the manager to identify just which barriers are causing the problem. Until you do that, you run a serious risk of wasting time, goodwill, effort, and money trying to solve the wrong problem. Emery Air Freight's container problem is a case in point. Once Emery's managers realized that the containers were being underused, they asked their three terminal supervisors to find the reason and suggest a solution.

As we know, the actual problem was that the workers simply didn't know they weren't peforming very well. Here are the answers that the three supervisors came up with:

Supervisor 1 Reason: The workers aren't being paid enough.

Solution: Raise wages across the board.

Cost of the solution: The workers would have been rewarded for poor performance.

Supervisor 2 Reason: The workers don't know what to do or how to do it.

Solution: Institute a training program.

Cost of the solution: Time wasted for the employees being trained to do something they already knew how to do.

Supervisor 3 Reason: The age, arrangement, and location of the building is wrong for the work to be done.

Solution: Tear down the building and build a new one.

Cost of the solution: A *lot* of money!

The actual solution to the problem was to make clear to the employees just what they were doing and what they should be doing. The cost of doing this was minimal.

"How did the Emery management know that the solutions offered by the three supervisors were all wrong?" Tim asked. "Just luck?"

"Something more than luck. Of course, before granting a raise or tearing down a building, they would have looked a lot deeper into the matter. But there are other ways to lead you to the right track. There's no guarantee, of course, that you're going to put your finger on the right answer every time, but there are some simple steps to point you in the right direction, or even do more than that.''

''Are you going to tell me? I'm ready to do it!''

FINDING THE CAUSE OF AND SOLUTION TO A PERFORMANCE PROBLEM

1. Determine what the performance level is right now. Look back at the goal and the time limit that you and your employees set when you began the project. Have you reached that goal on time? Are you approaching it at a reasonable pace or are you alarmingly behind schedule? If you have missed your deadline, or if you are way behind in approaching it, you have a performance problem.

2. Now place objective values on the desired increase in performance and on the cost of the solution you have in mind. For example, ''Getting this job out on time—and thereby keeping this valuable customer—would be worth $500,000 to the company. One way to get it out on time is to hire two temporary workers for the duration of the project. That solution to the problem would cost the company $3,000.''

3. Compare the cost of the solution ($3,000) to the value you expect it to bring ($500,000) and ask yourself, ''Is it worth it?'' (Yes!)

4. List all the tasks that must be performed in order to get the job done. Is it possible that, by improving performance in one particular task, you can bring total performance up to the desired level? Find that task and review your ROI for the employees who perform it. Revise it step by step, if necessary.

Ask yourself the following questions to help you determine which barriers to good performance you need to deal with:

Group 1 Barriers: Unclear Goals

- Do the employees know what is expected of them?
- Are the indicators clearly defined?
- Are the goals accepted by both employees and management?
- Do the employees have a clear idea of how their jobs relate to the company's mission?
- Have you expected too much too soon?

You can readily tell which answers indicate that the performance barrier is in

Group 1: The employees don't know what is expected of them. You're going to need to define the company's mission more clearly. You may also have to clarify the goals of your immediate section or of the individual worker. If there is a conflict between the mission and the goal, rework the goal to bring it in line with the company's purpose.

Group 2 Barriers: Lack of Skills

- Have the employees done the desired job in the past?
- Could they do it if their lives depended on it?
- Have there been any changes (large or small) in the way they are being asked to perform?
- Are their skills rusty?

The answers to these questions will help you decide whether or not your problem is with the second group of barriers—those arising when the employees don't know *how* to do something. The solution to this problem is clear: Arrange a training program or refresher course.

Group 3 Barriers: Apathy

- Are consequences weighted in favor of the desired behavior?
- Are there rewards contingent on behavior?
- Are rewards truly reinforcing?
- Are cultural norms interfering with performance?
- Has there been a change in the way rewards are given?
- Has a change in an employee's personal life changed that person's attitudes so that rewards that once were of value no longer seem desirable?

The answers to the questions in this group will tell you if you have a Group 3 barrier: Employees don't want to do the job. A balance-of-consequences analysis will help you learn how to change that feeling using reinforcers and punishers. Your analysis will show you where the former need to be added, the latter eliminated for the desired behavior.

Group 4 Barriers: Inadequate Materials

- Are procedures, forms, or red tape interfering with results?
- Do the employees need additional resources?
- Do the employees have the proper tools?

This should certainly tell you if you face a Group 4 barrier—lack of proper tools or procedures. Check all tools and equipment carefully and review the procedures. If procedures tend to be uselessly bureaucratic, with a lot of red tape and unnecessary paperwork, try to streamline them.

Group 5 Barriers: Poor Feedback

- Is feedback immediate, specific, accurate, and personal?
- Is feedback neutral?
- Are the employees being given information concerning their performance?

A lack of accurate and adequate feedback will show up when you ask yourself these questions. Be sure you make feedback available regularly, and make certain it is full, accurate, and nonjudgmental.

- Are the employees' capacities greater than what the job demands?
- Would their talents be better used elsewhere?
- Do they have the physical and mental capacity to perform at the desired level?

Group 6 Barriers: Qualification Problems

After asking yourself these questions, you'll realize that the employee either does not have the ability to do the job or is overqualified for it. The solution? Transfer the person to a job that better matches his or her abilities, or restructure the present job. If the problem is in this category, the manager would do well to go back and review the procedures that put this employee into an unsuitable job in the first place. What can be changed to prevent this from happening in the future?

Going over these lists of questions can be very helpful; often that's all you need do to pinpoint the problem and determine a solution.

"What if the questions don't give me enough clues?" Tim asked. "What if I need more than that? Am I stuck?"

"No, you're not. If you think about it a minute, you'll realize that there's one excellent source of information about the problem that you haven't tapped yet."

"Hmmm. The employee?"

"You got it."

"Can you recommend any kind of tried-and-true way to ask the employee about the problem? Do I just go up to one of my people and say, 'Hey, Shirley, you aren't doing so hot. What's the trouble?'"

"Not quite. All through our discussions we've been giving you specific goals, and we've talked a lot about how you can reach them."

"You're giving me support."

We laughed. "That's about it. Anyhow, this is no exception."

There's a pattern for an interview with an employee whose performance is falling short of what it should be. The "aha!" is that the employee is not responsible for

- knowing what's expected
- how he or she is doing
- having the skills
- eliminating organization barriers
- offering rewards, recognition, instruction

Who is? We'll look at this question in the next chapter.

Support—Talking It Out

Do you handle poor performance this way?

MANNY   Hey! Temper, temper, temper.

TED   Never mind that. I'm up to here with this stuff!

MANNY   Yeah, I noticed. That's what I came in to talk to you about. That report you wrote on last month's work—Ted, I don't know. I just can't believe how bad it is. This is the end of the quarter, and I'm supposed to tell my management what we've accomplished here in the lab. The report—and the two before it, too—just don't say anything. From what I can gather, you've been doing experiments two and three times when one should have been enough, just because you goofed up the first time.

TED   What if I have?

MANNY   You used to be so terrific about ways to improve the products. What happened? There's nothing like that here. Where did you lose your steam?

TED   Right here at this desk, that's where I lost my steam! Do you realize that I've had to train three new techs in the last three months? Do you think that doesn't take time? <u>Plus</u> the department is three times as big as it used to be. New people coming in all the time, more sophisticated and complicated tests, more equipment to check, more meetings, more reports! When in hell am I supposed to do everything? And you expect me to give you pretty monthly reports, too?

MANNY   Well, I expect something from you besides what I got. You used to be our most creative lab person—always bursting with new ideas. You sure as hell aren't that way any more! You better watch it, Ted, or you're going to find yourself in real trouble!

TED   You know what you can do!

Or do you handle poor performance this way?

MANNY   Got a minute, Ted?

TED   These days I've <u>never</u> got a minute. But I'll take a minute—or more if you want it. Have a seat, Manny.

MANNY   Thanks, Ted. I know you're busy. Ted, I've been going over your last monthly reports. Remember, when we talked about it before, you said you'd expand them. We really need a detailed summary of all the test results, your conclusions based on the results, and suggestions for new experiments.

TED   I <u>remember</u> all that, Manny, but I'm loaded down with other work. I can't do the impossible. I know the report could be better, but do you realize how long it took me to write it the way it is?

MANNY   You mean the problem is lack of time, right?

TED   Well, I guess...

MANNY   It's <u>not</u> time?

TED   Oh, sure it is, but it's more than that. Look, Manny, you made me a supervisor because I'm good out there on the floor. When I'm out there, I get ideas just working with the people doing the tests. But now I'm more of an administrator than a line person. I have to spend about half of every day here at the desk, just trying to keep up with all the paperwork I have to do. No wonder I can't get good ideas! No wonder I can't handle <u>anything</u> well anymore.

MANNY   I see. I know there's a lot more administrative work, Ted. What you're telling me is that it's not just that you're too busy to do everything well. You're also not doing the kind of work you want to do, and that makes you feel fed up and frustrated and not really caring about performance. Is that it?

TED   Yeah. Yes, I'm afraid that's pretty much it.

MANNY   Okay. So the way to solve that would be if we could take some of the paperwork off your hands, right?

TED   You bet! If I could just get someone to help with this stuff, I could spend more time out on the floor. That's what I really want. In fact, I've been thinking about quitting and finding a job where I could really do active testing.

MANNY   A job like that probably wouldn't pay as much.

TED   I wouldn't have to spend half the day on my bottom pushing a pen around, though.

MANNY   Well, I think we can solve it right here in the company. Have you got anyone in your unit who could do some of the report?

TED   Absolutely. Dan and Lucy both could handle the weekly and monthly summaries.

MANNY   Can you spare them from their regular work for enough time to write up those summaries?

TED   Sure I could.

MANNY   How about if we do that, then? Let Dan and Lucy do the summaries.

TED   It'd be great!

MANNY   I'm still counting on you for the conclusions, Ted. And I'm looking forward to getting some good suggestions for new products and procedures from you.

TED   Manny, I think I can promise you you'll get them as long as I don't have to play Mr. Deskman.

Problems are things to be solved, not opportunities to fix blame.

CHAPTER 11

WE'RE IN THIS TOGETHER: THE CHANGE INTERVIEW

"It's only when you're face to face that you're able to see eye to eye."

—*Jerome Kurtz*

ROI, THE TWO-TO-FOUR-MINUTE FEEDBACK SESSION, behavior modification, reinforcement, balance-of-consequence analysis—all are techniques for applying the first four basic principles of positive management: mission, goals, feedback, and rewards. There's a technique for offering your support as well, for letting your employees know that you're there to help them, not to punish them.

"Look," Tim Stone said to us the next time we saw him. "I've learned a lot from our talks, and I'm really looking foward to giving positive management a try. But right now—just as a practice run, you might say—I'd like to tell you about something that came up at my place and the way I handled it. Then you can tell me whether I behaved like a true positive manager. Okay?"

"Good idea," we said. "What's the story?"

"As you know, we make audio and videotapes, and even though our products cost more than our competitors', they're technically a lot better. Our customers are willing to pay more for quality and advanced technology. Now, I have a rep named Brian, who sells both audio and videotapes, and for a long time, he had a great record; in fact he was our best sales rep."

"Then two things happened. First, the cost of materials went up. Then our new contract with the union called for big pay hikes. As a result, we had to raise the price of all our tapes. That meant that the differential between our price and our competitors' got even greater. And then our biggest competition dropped a bomb: They came out with an audio tape that is technically a great improvement over what they'd been selling. It still isn't up to ours, but it's a lot closer. And I don't know how they managed it, but they didn't raise the price on those audios!

"Well, that kind of played hell with Brian's accounts. Some customers stayed with him, but even they are buying their audios from the other company and only the videos from Brian. Others have even stopped buying our videotapes; I guess they preferred one-stop shopping. Of course, Brian hasn't lost everybody; our videos are still head and shoulders above every one else's technically, but what was once an easy, relaxed selling job has turned into tough, punishing work—and Brian doesn't like it. I realized recently that he's been concentrating on selling the video, where the job is easier.

"I kept in mind all you and I have been talking about, and I tried to figure out how to work through this problem. I went over all the questions you gave me, and sure enough, the answers showed me what kind of barriers were keeping Brian from performing the way he should.

"First, he didn't *want* to sell audiotapes. I did a balance-of-consequences analysis to figure out how I could reinforce his selling them and eliminate some of the punishing consequences of his trying to sell them. Well, anyhow, *he* thought they were punishers, so I took them into account."

"That's good," we told him. "You're remembering that when you list the rewards and punishers for an employee, you've got to put yourself in that person's place and evaluate the consequences from his or her point of view."

"Right. I did remember that. Then I discovered another kind of barrier that was preventing Brian from performing well: I learned that, beyond a certain point, he really didn't know *how* to sell quality against price. Remember, now—even though our competitor has improved the quality of his lower-priced audio tapes, ours are still much better."

"What did you do then?"

"I decided the best thing to do was have a talk with Brian. He made it clear that the reason he doesn't want to sell the audiotapes is that he doesn't think he can compete at so much higher a price. Well, I can't lower the price, but I do have the authority to set special prices for special packages, for people who buy in large quantities. So together, Brian and I worked out some special deals. Then we thought of some incentives he could use to entice the smaller account into coming to us—or staying with us.

"I told him I would arrange for him to take a sales training program, where they'd give him some pointers on selling quality against price. He was very pleased about that.

"Finally, I asked him if he wanted me to go with him on some of his tougher calls just to give a fresh perspective on how he is going about it. Brian agreed, he liked the idea. Of course, since then I've made it a point to 'reinforce' him every time he makes an audiotape sale. I even do it when he gets an expression of interest from a new prospect."

We congratulated Tim on his actions. He'd learned his lesson well. "We've worked out a procedure for cooperative talks with employees who have problems," we told him. "We call it the *change interview.*"

When an employee has a problem the manager's first impulse may be to jump on the unfortunate person with criticism—negative feedback. But that, as we've explained, has many disadvantages, some of which will boomerang and create a managerial problem. As we said earlier, the employee quickly comes to associate the manager with negative comment. When that happens, employees become less responsible for their actions. And there's always the danger, too, that the negative feedback will somehow reinforce the undesired behavior, especially if the employee craves attention in any form.

Because of all the disadvantages of negative feedback, we've been encouraging you to avoid it. You'll do best to ignore poor performance and concentrate on giving the employee positive reinforcement in the hope that

that alone will do the trick. Unfortunately, this doesn't always work. You can't ignore poor performance indefinitely; sometimes you have to take the direct approach.

The president of a very large manufacturing concern takes a wise approach. This man assumes that when his people aren't doing a good job, it's not because they don't want to. Instead, something is preventing them from doing their best to serve their company and its customers. Therefore, reasons this executive, it's up to every manager to notice when an employee is not performing up to standard, try to discover what is getting in the way of good performance, and negotiate a change in the person's performance. To allow an employee to continue doing the job poorly is a failure of integrity on the manager's part. The employee should be told.

This is a critical belief—a belief that shows trust in and respect for a company's employees and a willingness on management's part to deal face to face with them.

THE CHANGE INTERVIEW

That's where the change interview comes in. It takes the sting out of negative feedback, because you and your employee will face the problem together, and the employee will have a say in determining the future course of the work. The change interview is an example of managerial support at its best, and it can be a powerful influence on an employee's peformance.

Before you meet with the employee, take these preliminary actions:

- Go through the questions designed to help you pinpoint the barriers to satisfactory performance.
- Work out the discrepancy between the actual performance and the desired performance, according to the goals you've agreed on.
- Weigh the value of the increased productivity against any possible cost of increasing it.

Note of caution: Employees regard a private talk with the boss as a pretty grave business, so save it for a genuinely serious problem. Don't take a cavalier attitude toward this technique. Used too often—or for minor problems—it will quickly lose its effectiveness.

Now, before you plunge into the change interview, let's examine the four steps this technique comprises. (You'll realize that this is a variation of the two-to-four-minute feedback session.) We'll capsulize the four steps first and then discuss each one in detail. Here they are:

1. Describe the performance discrepancy for the employee in brief, factual, neutral terms. Identify your role as providing support where it is requested.

2. Ask questions that look to the future and that call for the employee to identify specific solutions. Avoid "why" or "who" questions that might be interpreted as an attempt to fix blame. Also avoid leading questions.

3. Reinforce positive planning and outlook. Ignore excuses.

4. Gain agreement on what the barrier is to increased performance and how to clear it. If necessary, agree on a new goal and set a review meeting.

Those steps are certainly simple enough, but they are so important that it will pay us to elaborate on them one at a time.

In Step 1 your job is to make clear to the employee that his or her performance has fallen short in a certain area. Okay, that part is easy. The hard part is to make absolutely certain the person knows you're there to help, not to criticize or blame; your job is to support the employee, to help analyze the difficulties, and to assist in planning future changes. Letting the person know that the two of you have a mutual interest in the success of the project and that you are working together toward an agreed-upon goal will avoid your putting the employee on the defensive.

In Step 2, you and the employee, together, will explore the changes the employee can make in the future to eliminate the problem and improve job performance. Your willingness to help the person find a solution to the problem should take the curse off the negative feedback you had to provide at the beginning of your discussion. At this step, avoid "why" and "who" questions; they'll only alarm the employee. "*Why* did you send the orders out three days late?" "*Who* told you there was no need to hurry?" A person faced with questions like these will assume you're looking for a whipping boy. Avoid leading questions, too. Let the employee volunteer information.

The change interview works best when it focuses on future action, so ask the employee to tell you what needs to be done and how you can contribute to reaching the goal. You might say something like this: "It looks as if it's going to take more than one person to get this job done. What can I do to help you get it done?"

Again, the warning: Stay away from any statement or question that smacks of blame-laying or that is likely to produce an alibi. That kind of talk will not solve the problem. In fact, the hostility it usually evokes can exacerbate the problem.

Don't ask questions to which you already know the answers. You aren't out to entrap anyone; you're trying to work with the employee to solve a problem.

"Now," asked Tim, "you've created a Catch-22, haven't you? You can't solve the problem if you can't identify it, and you can't identify it without asking the employee what it is, and that's not a good idea. Explain your way out of that one."

"You're right: It's *not* a good idea to ask the employee what the problem is. And you're wrong: You *can* identify a problem without asking the employee to do it for you. You see, Tim, the employee almost always knows what the problem is. When you ask what needs to be done in the future, you're asking the employee to propose a solution. Once he or she has done so, you can easily identify the problem from the solution."

"Suppose the employee says this: 'I think the solution to this problem would be for me to switch tasks with Sharon on this step. I can get the orders ready faster than she can—and *know* they'll be accurate; and she can handle the boys in the stock room better than I can.' What does that tell you, Tim?"

"I concede the point," Tim said. "We had the right people doing the wrong chores."

In Step 3 your job is to reinforce positive planning and outlook and ignore excuses. At this point, greet any positive planning with enthusiasm and praise; reinforce positive thinking and positive solutions.

"And what about negative comments?" Tim asked.

"If possible, ignore them—but there's an exception to that. If the employee brings up the gripes and complaints and excuses in a very emotional way, it's best to let it all come out. Just listen to the tale of woe. You don't have to agree with the employee's version of the cause of the problem, but you should sympathize. Acknowledge that the employee has a right to be upset.

"Then, when the air is cleared, be positive. Ask questions that focus on the future and on solutions. Do not make negative comments. You might have to allow for a cooling-off time between the emotional outpouring and the serious discussion about how the job is to be handled in the future. That's okay. Put the interview off until another day if necessary."

"What if I ask how performance could be improved in the future and the employee comes up with a solution that's impractical or stupid or prohibitively expensive? What do I do then? How can I reject the idea without discouraging the person who suggested it?"

"You can almost always find something good to say about a suggestion—something you can compliment, even if it's only the fact that the employee actually offered it. Don't be discouraging; be positive. Point out anything that is right about the idea. Then build on that. Share your own knowledge and ideas. Then use the shaping technique to help the employee come up with a better solution."

In Step 4, you try to gain the employee's agreement. After you've discussed the problem with the employee and talked over possible solutions, settle on one that is acceptable both to you and the employee. Set a new goal. Be sure to include a time limit; it could be a date for another meeting, where you'll go over what has been accomplished.

Make it clear to the employee exactly what the consequences will be if the desired improvement doesn't take place. But be sure as well to describe the personal and organizational rewards that will be won if the goal is reached. Finally, go back and recap the agreement you and the employee have just made. List the steps that the two of you have agreed to take; repeat the time limit you've established, and review the intermediate steps that will serve as checkpoints along the way.

"You know what I am?" Tim said. "I'm stuffed with information."

We laughed. "Put it to good use, okay?"

"I intend to."

How Tim—and you—will use the management wheel in your own organization is the subject of our last chapter.

Talking It Out

Keeping in mind the purpose of the change interview—solving a problem, not laying blame—let's listen in on a conversation between an account manager in an advertising agency and an account executive whose proposal for a series of television commercials has just been rejected by a client. Laurie, the manager, studied communication with Dr. Nick Wesler, a psychology professor and the director of the Management Communication Institute in Washington, D.C. From Dr. Wesler, Laurie learned to conduct an open, relaxed interview and to lead the employee to solve the problem rather than simply to complain about it.

ROB   Laurie, I've got bad news. Butler Technology turned down five of the six scripts I showed them. I'm just about ready to give up on those people. They're never satisfied with anything. They complained about the first series of scripts I showed them because there wasn't enough humor in them. Now that I've revised them and made them lighter, they're still complaining.

LAURIE   Exactly what did they say about the scripts, Rob?

ROB   They liked the one about the parents who buy a home computer for their son and daughter, but they hated all the others.

LAURIE   Did they say exactly what they objected to in the other five? Those scripts seemed really good to me, but of course the manufacturers of the computer look at things quite differently than we do. Did they say exactly what they objected to in the other five commercials?

ROB   They say the scripts aren't "real" enough. Can you believe that? How much reality can I get into a ninety-second TV commercial, for Pete's sake? Those people know everything about computers, but they don't know anything at all about TV commercials.

LAURIE   They said the scripts weren't real enough? Do you think they meant you didn't provide enough concrete information about the product?

ROB   I don't think they know what they mean. They're just bending over backwards to be disagreeable.

LAURIE   But they liked the one about the parents and children. That one, as I remember, did include a good deal of helpful information about the home computer. Do you think that's why they accepted it?

ROB   I don't know. Maybe. Do you think I should rewrite the others along the same lines and present them to the clients once more?

LAURIE   You know the Butler Tech people better than I do, Rob. What do you think? Have you any idea what they mean when they say the scripts aren't "real" enough?

ROB   Maybe I do, Laurie. You see, I worked really hard to create real people using home computers in realistic ways, so I can't accept the Butler people's comment that the scripts aren't real enough. I don't think that's what they really mean. It's just something they said because they can't put their finger on exactly what they don't like about the scripts.

LAURIE   Which is...

ROB   Which is, I think, the language.

LAURIE   You mean the language used by the characters in the commercials? The parents and kids, for example? And the voice-over?

ROB   Right. When we were discussing the proposal, I noticed that the clients used terms I wasn't familiar with—buzzwords, I guess you'd call them. I did a lot of research on the products, and I understand them thoroughly, but I don't know the buzzwords that computer users toss around when they talk among themselves.

LAURIE   I see what you mean, Rob. You're saying that the clients regard the scripts as unrealistic when it's actually only the vocabulary, not the scripts themselves that they don't like.

ROB   Right. That's it exactly. The clients got the impression that I didn't understand the computer, whereas I really do understand it thoroughly. I guess I created that misunderstanding myself by not becoming familiar with the jargon before I put the scenes down on paper. What do you think I should do now?

LAURIE   Why don't you tell me what _you_ think you should do?

ROB   Okay. I'd like to spend all day tomorrow at Butler Technology, but instead of asking a million questions, as I did the first time I went out there, I'd just like to hang around and listen to the way computer people talk. Maybe I'll spend some time in the company lunch room just soaking up the vocabulary.

LAURIE   Sounds good, Rob. What will you do after you visit the plant?

ROB   I'll get to work on those scripts again, and I'll rework the dialogue until it sounds authentic.

LAURIE Using the same situations and characters?

ROB   Yes. The Butler people had no specific objections to those. In fact they made a point of telling me they liked the wide range of situations and the appeal to all different kinds of people.

LAURIE Rob, I think you've solved your problem already. Why don't you set things up with the Butler people for your visit tomorrow? If you can get the information you need in just one day, how soon do you think you could have another proposal ready?

ROB   It can be fairly soon. I won't have to do any major reworking or come up with any brand-new concepts. It'll be just a matter of making the words come out of the characters' mouths differently, so it won't take all that long.

LAURIE Great. Let's get together when you've worked over, say, two of the rejected scripts. If we both agree that the clients will accept them, maybe you can present just those two for Butler's approval. That way, you'll know exactly how to proceed on the rest of the series.

ROB   That's a good idea. When I finish those two scripts, we'll also be able to draw up a schedule for the rest of the work. If all goes well, I should be able to deliver the whole package by the end of the month.

LAURIE I'm sure you'll come up with something they really like this time, Rob, now that you understand the problem.

ROB   Thanks for your help. I was almost desperate for a solution to this one. I just couldn't decide what to do to please the clients.

LAURIE The clients made it hard on you, because they weren't specific about what they didn't like about the scripts. You had to figure that out pretty much yourself. That sort of thinking is maddening, but it happens all the time. People very often don't know exactly what it is that they object to; they just know that something is bothering them. That puts you in a difficult spot, since it's hard for you to be objective when people are criticizing you and picking your work apart. Sometimes it helps to talk it out with someone else, someone who's less directly involved than you are. That way you can see more clearly what your choices are. It was nice talking to you, Rob. I'll look forward to seeing those reworked scripts.

CHAPTER 12

MAKING IT REAL, MAKING IT WORK: GETTING BEHIND THE MANAGEMENT WHEEL

The whole is greater than the sum of the parts.
—*Christian von Ehrenfels*

THE MANAGEMENT WHEEL IS A COMBINATION OF FIVE interlocking, interdependent elements that constitute your key to effective management. You make them your own by applying them to your own work place.

The next time we saw Tim Stone, he was in high spirits. "Well," he said, laughing, "I guess now you've taught me everything you know."

"Just about," we told him. "But now comes the real test—putting the knowledge to use in your own job. Creating a climate conducive to positive, productive behavior and keeping it going. Managers tend to be great initiators, missionaries, and goal-setters. They're selective on those qualities. But often they're not too great at rewards, reinforcement, feedback, and support."

"I've been trying to keep the positive things going, a little bit at a time, here and there, as we've been having these talks. But I realize that that isn't really the way to go about it."

We agreed. "It's often best to choose a relatively small project, and apply all the principles you have learned to it, step by step. Don't be overly ambitious; remember, this is a tryout. You're trying to learn from it more than anything else. And if you can make this work, you'll find it easier to go on to really significant actions."

"I've got something picked out to use as a guinea-pig project," Tim said. "It's something we've been fooling around with for a while, but it is a small part of what we do, and other things have been more urgent. If I use it as the subject of my experiment in positive management, I'll accomplish two things: getting the project straightened out and making my test run."

"Good. Before you start, we're going to give you a list of things to watch out for. We think they'll help you set up the whole project and get it started in the right way. Some of them you know already, and have even acted on."

Before you start the management wheel rolling, check these points out:

- The people at the top must be committed to the project. That means you and those of your supervisors who are concerned with the project.
- The project should not be too big or too complex.
- The design of the project should command a lot of attention.
- Manager and subordinates should agree on standards of performance.
- Subordinates must be involved at every stage of the project.
- Build feedback right into the program, and collect data on the results. Design the feedback systems carefully.
- Be sure the employee or manager responsible for analyzing the per-

formance is familiar with the techniques of the activity concerned. If not, arrange for a training program.

- Emphasize the techniques of positive reinforcement.
- Give the project time to show results; don't be impatient; don't push the program too far. You can't expect to see results for at least two to six months after initiating it.
- Be sure to take into account other systems at work in your company that are beyond your control: salary, budget, management appraisal.
- Remember, positive management is not a fad for this year; it's a continuing process and leadership tool.

"Okay, Tim," we said. "That's your list of do's and don'ts. Tell us something. What work unit will your program apply to? The whole company? Or your department, or just part of it?"

"One section of my department. The work itself doesn't involve any other part of the company except sales, in a way. Let me tell you about it.

"Some months ago, one of the engineers in our design department—a bright young woman named Susan Sommers—suggested that if we made certain changes in the design of one of our microcircuits, we could use it to adapt a special-purpose scanner to do a lot more different things. It seemed like a really good idea, and we had it checked out by various people in the specifications office and elsewhere, and it looked like it would work.

"It still looks that way, but it's turning out to be a much more complex job to get this ready for the production department than we thought it would. Meanwhile, we've given the marketing people a good idea of what the new circuitry will do when it's worked out, but they haven't anything to show— and we don't want it to sound like they're trying to sell a lot of empty promises. The back orders are piling up, and if we can't get into production pretty soon, the whole project is going to have to be scrapped. But I think we're going to be able to pull it off. The people on it are still very enthusiastic, and they're experienced enough to know that things don't always go smoothly, but that that doesn't mean they won't come out all right in the end."

"Does the project relate to your company's mission?"

"Oh, yes. We see our mission as tailoring our products to our customer's special needs, and this certainly will do that. We'll be able to adapt several ways, to meet the needs of different customers."

"Then there's a clear relation between the work and the company mission, isn't there? That's lucky; you won't have as much trouble getting the connection over to your people. Sometimes that's a real problem. Especially if the mission is far removed from the day-to-day work people are doing. How do you plan to get over to them the idea that they have a share in the company's mission?"

THE POSITIVE MANAGER · 173

"Well," Tim said, "of course, we've been talking about that all along, and I've been plugging the idea. I think they already feel pretty much a part of the mission. That's explained in our orientation program for new employees; any training courses they take, same thing—get the message in. I've talked to the personnel department about hammering away—in a subtle way, of course, if you *can* hammer in a subtle way—at the company's mission in the newsletter and in bulletins whenever they can. I put stuff up on the bulletin board—little jokes and whatnot, all directed to that end. And sometimes at department meetings, instead of just talking at my staff people, I get them to do a little role-playing. I get one of the people to be the customer, for instance, so they'll get some insight from the customer's point of view about what the public expects from the company. It all adds up."

Tim is right. And it's always easier to communicate mission if the norms that exist in the culture of the work place don't militate against it.

Identify the norms in your work place. One way to spot them is to ask a new employee to tell the difference between the former job and the present one.

Get your employees together to talk about what norms exist. Try to overcome the "supernorm" that says, "Don't talk about anything we do to management."

Take a good look at the norms that exist. Separate them into those that contribute to mission and those that work against it. Strengthen the former; try to eliminate the latter. Begin by eliminating the least controversial norm. Which is the least controversial counterproductive norm in your workplace—the easiest one to try to change?

"The next step is to set some work goals. Remember how important it is for the goal to be personally important to the employee."

"Yeah, I remember that. I've been taking your advice, and getting to know my employees better. I've gone out bowling with them a few times, and we've had some really good talks over a beer or two afterward. At first, I was nervous about that. I thought they wouldn't like the boss horning in on their after-work pleasure. But they seemed pleased to have me around, and I'm glad I did it. Also, I didn't forget that if I want them to be honest with me, I've got to be honest with them. You should have heard some of the stuff I told them. I really let down my hair about what's important to me and what isn't."

"Good. Now you're in a good spot to set some goals, along with your people, goals that mean something." The following are guidelines for goals. They must be:

- realistic
- understandable and specific
- measurable
- related to specific actions
- subject to a time limit
- written down
- compatible with all other goals
- acceptable to all parties concerned
- kept up to date
- accompanied by built-in feedback
- rewarded

We reminded Tim of the 20–80 rule, which says that 20 percent of what people do is responsible for 80 percent of their effectiveness. Here's a way to apply that rule:

> **List all the important behaviors the employees in your program are going through when they do the job. Then pick out the 20 percent of those behaviors that lead to 80 percent of the effective results. Concentrate on improving those.**

Use ROI to set the goals:

- Identify Responsibilities
- Break each down into Objectives
- Establish Indicators for each objective

"And," Tim said, "if I remember correctly, do that together with my employees. Right?"

"That's right. After you've done the preliminary work and drafted the three steps—R, O, I—meet with your people and go over what you've come up with. Make the organization's goals very clear. Be sure to tell the employees that you know the areas where you will have to provide support, and that you're ready to provide it. Be sure that everyone agrees on the goals, the objectives and the indicators, and adjust them if there are valid objections to the way you've set them up. Or if someone has a better idea. Remember, this is a cooperative effort.

"Then set up a schedule to review the indicators regularly. The employees are responsible for them, but you are responsible for overseeing them.

"Okay. Now you've got that set up. What are you going to do next?"

"Feedback."

"Have you got any plans for that?"

"Yep. We've got the employees on this project divided into teams. I'm going to have each team keep a graph of weekly progress. And I'll keep a sharp eye on those graphs myself, so I can catch anything that might turn into a problem and talk to the people involved before it goes too far."

"That sounds good. You've remembered a lot of what we've been talking about."

"Sure I have," Tim said. "It impressed me a lot. I'm gung-ho about trying this program out. If it works on this project, I'm going to use it in all the different sections."

We advised Tim to try to restrict the feedback to the effective 20 percent actions areas instead of trying to get it on every single step. We told him to be sure that the feedback came as quickly as possible after the performance.

"Then use the Two-to-Four-Minute Feedback Session to get at the problem."

"Sure, I intend to. I think that when we get this going, it's bound to be really effective. I'm really looking forward to trying it out."

"That's an asset, Tim. Enthusiasm has a way of being contagious."

How do you plan to monitor feedback in *your* work place?

"After that," Tim said, "when I know how people are performing, I'll reinforce the behavior I want to see kept up. I may have to dig pretty deep to find some positive behavior to reinforce, at first, but I'm remembering what Skinner said—that behavior is a function of its consequences. So I've got to keep those consequences positive if I want to see positive behavior, right? You've really convinced me of the value of intangible rewards. I have no control over pay and fringe benefits, but you showed me there's a lot I *can* give my people. The pat on the back, added responsibility, a complimentary memo every now and then . . ."

"Those things work."

"I believe it! I'm depending on the balance-of-consequences analysis. It tells you what to do in such a logical and sensible way; it's a great guide to positive management, like all the other shortcuts you've given me. Using the balance-of-consequences analysis, and remembering that people respond to consequences, not antecedents, I'll know just how to change things to make the balance come out on the side of effective action."

We pointed out that aside from reinforcement, there were other techniques of behavior modification.

"Sure. Like punishment—but you try like hell to avoid using that. It's better to reinforce the behavior you are trying to get than to punish the behavior you don't want. And you only use punishment if the employee is robbing the company or threating to blow the place up."

He went on to describe extinction, and then shaping. "Sounds like I'm on my way, doesn't it?" Tim said. "I've talked about mission and evaluated the norms of my own work place. I've set goals and objectives and indicators. I've arranged for feedback. I'm aware that I have to reinforce my people by giving them rewards—praise, responsibility, authority, changes in their routine..."

"What's left?"

"What's left is my job—being ready and willing to support my employees all the way and being sure I know when they need support, even if they don't tell me, even if they don't know they need it. And I mean anywhere along the way, not just at the beginning when a new employee comes in. I have to encourage them to come to me for support by telling them that I'll think better of them for doing it."

"You've got a tool for locating the trouble, too, so that when you give support, you'll be giving it for the right problem."

"I know. I've already memorized that list of telltale questions. And I know how to go about the change interview. It's a lot like the two-to-four minute feedback session, except that I've got to tell my employees where they're falling short, and I've got to do it in such a way that they'll know I'm not trying to fix the blame on anybody; that we're looking together for the source of the trouble."

"That's great, Tim. All in all, what is the most important thing you've learned?"

"Gee, that's the hardest question you've asked me in all this time. I've learned so much—changed my whole outlook. I guess it could be summed up in *thinking positive.* Like that bit in the feedback session, where a criticism was turned into a positive plan for the future. I think that kind of thing is neat and good and important. Not just that, but the whole positive outlook behind it."

> **What is the one most important thing *you* have learned?**
> **What do you want to try the most?**
> **What are the present strengths you want to maximize?**

Think about the five elements of the management wheel: mission, goals, feedback, reward, and support. What is your weakest link? How has this weakness affected your department's work? What can you do to change it?

Always be aware of the people you supervise. Watch their reactions to what happens at work. You now have tools to analyze their responses. When you sense that they're reacting negatively, you can find the weak link in the management wheel and correct it. When you get a good feeling, strengthen what you're doing right.

"One thing we know," we told Tim. "You won't have any trouble creating an atmosphere where your employees are willing to communicate information. Your people, from what we've heard, know that you're interested in helping to make their jobs more rewarding—that you're interested in *them*, as people."

"It wasn't always that way," Tim said. "I started out thinking that my people had decent salaries and good working conditions, and that's all they needed to want to perform well. So I couldn't understand why they weren't performing as well as I thought they could. But talking to you has changed my attitude, and my people have changed along with me. They know that I'm looking at them and their jobs in a whole new way, and they're responding to that."

"That's pretty positive reinforcement for *us*, Tim," we said. "We'll look forward to hearing how your project goes. We're pretty sure it's going to be successful. You're going about it in just the right way. If you do have problems, you'll be able to solve them. You've got your employees behind you already, and that's a positive step. If you stay positive all the way down the line, Tim, you can't go wrong."

Later on, when Tim and I were having coffee in the company cafeteria after the lunch crowd had cleared out, I asked him, "Why did you become a manager, Tim?"

"I don't know exactly," he answered. "I couldn't pinpoint any one reason. But it's not for just the money and the four-week vacations. After all, when I was having trouble getting performance from my unit, before you helped me get on the right track, I was pulling down the same pay and the same perks. And it's not like someone was pressuring me to improve my division's performance. But I just didn't like my work in those days. It was darn frustrating!"

That ties in with what we've found out about the best managers. Wilson Learning Corporation interviewed fifty managers who were singled out for their excellence. The interviews proved that, in spite of what many believe, these people didn't regard their jobs as just a means of earning more money and perks. When we asked them why they wanted to become managers, we realized that the roots of their concern with their jobs went back to their own experiences under outstanding managers.

Time and time again we heard the phrase "the best manager I ever had." The enthusiasm and excellence of almost all of the managers we interviewed could be traced back to an earlier manager who served as mentor and model. Invariably these managers encouraged their protégés and helped them learn to take responsibility and make decisions on their own. These younger managers, in other words, had the advantage of having seen the way outstanding older managers handled the job. When they themselves won supervisory positions, they had an example to follow. They could act, therefore, in a spirit of cooperation rather than one of coercion; their effectiveness sprang from leadership rather than authoritarianism. They could be *positive*. They could encourage their own employees to take responsibility and to make decisions on their own, just as they themselves had been able to do.

In this way, good managers are passing on a tradition of excellence—one whose impact is far-reaching and must have a positive effect on the whole climate of American business.

Talking It Out

Arthur and Steve, the two managers at the Wright-Jones Corporation—the farm machinery company—are relaxing over lunch at an outdoor table on the grounds near the plant.

ARTHUR I think I've known you long enough, Steve, to be confident that you won't say, "I told you so," if I admit you were right about something.

STEVE What's that?

ARTHUR That series of management seminars you encouraged me to attend. You were absolutely right all the way down the line, Steve. I've been putting to use the principles I learned in those sessions, and the results in my department have been amazing.

STEVE That doesn't surprise me. I've been seeing an awful lot of smiling designers walking around here lately. They always seem to be gesturing wildly to one another, making suggestions for improvements on this or that farm machine, or delivering enthusiastic reports of their most recent visit to some area farm where our products are in use. It looks to me as if your people couldn't be happier.

ARTHUR Thanks to my new understanding of effective management techniques—and thanks also to you for making me see how important it is to keep my ideas up to date. I'm afraid I was well on my way to becoming a fossil of sorts, Steve. While you managed to change and grow over these twenty-five years, I somehow allowed myself to remain stuck in the 1950s when the work place was nothing more than a big room in which you had to spend eight hours a day if you wanted to keep on eating. It seems incredible to me now—after talking with you and putting the seminar principles to work in my department—I simply failed to see how the work world was changing.

STEVE So tell me what else you've done in your department—besides change your designers' goals from short-range planning of details to long-range whole-machine designing.

ARTHUR I've stopping thinking of myself as the manager of a department, and started acting like a manager of people—individual workers, each one different, each of them gifted in his or her way, every man and woman with an individual set of needs, interests, and desires. I've stopping worrying about what the top brass thinks of me, and I've started concentrating on ways to make my people perform to the best of their ability—which is, by the way, more impressive than I ever realized. We've got ideas bouncing around in those offices that are going to revolutionize the farm machinery industry and keep this company way out ahead of the pack.

STEVE   And feed a few million more people? Don't forget the company mission, Arthur—putting efficient machines on the farms means putting more food on people's tables.

ARTHUR   Yes, and that's another point I learned to stress. I used to take it for granted that everyone who worked here understood that he or she was part of the general effort to feed the people of the world. Well, I was wrong. The designers knew it, of course, because their work kept them directly involved with the products. But my clerical staff had no feeling for the company mission at all. Putting them in touch with it was the first thing I set my hand to when I came back from the seminar.

STEVE   Those people really are an integral part of the company effort. Every column of figures they add up and every letter they type contributes to the production of the machinery that plants and harvests crops all over the world. Once you look at the job from where they stand, you can see the problems they face, and then you can sit down with them and work toward a solution.

ARTHUR   That's where the seminars helped me the most. I'm afraid I used to see my people as facilitators of my own work; now I see myself as a facilitator of their work. I'm finding out new ways to make their work more satisfying as well as more efficient, and in the meantime my department is flourishing as never before. I've stopped imposing my ideas on people, and I've begun to ask their opinions and implement their suggestions whenever I can. And I praise them more now.

STEVE   And you know exactly where your department is going, don't you? I saw your list of goals posted on the bulletin board. You really picked up on that bit of advice. Those goals are absolutely realistic, uncontradictory, and immediately measurable. Your people ought to be quite happy with them.

ARTHUR   Well, of course they are. They helped me formulate the goals. You certainly don't think I'd impose a set of arbitrary goals on my staff, do you? Certainly not, after all I've learned in the past few months.

STEVE   Arthur, I'm afraid our lunch hour is going to come to a sudden end. Look behind you—three of your designers are headed this way, waving their arms and shouting, as usual. I have a feeling they're about to revolutionize the farm machine industry before my very eyes. I'll see you later, buddy. I'm going to escape to my nice quiet shipping department while I still can get away.